The Flight and Flying collection is an excellent resource for students and seasoned aviators. Author Alex Burton's work is an excellent contribution to the field. The strong academic foundation of the essays is further enhanced by the many real-world examples. This combination of practical application, theory and solid research are presented in clear, accessible prose that will appeal to a wide range of readers.

Dr. Kori Street, Chair, Aviation Department
Bissett School of Aviation
Mount Royal University
Calgary, Alberta

"Alex Burton has an engaging style of writing that is educational, yet you forget that you're learning as it is so enjoyable to read. His personal experiences and passion for aviation are seamlessly interwoven with academic knowledge throughout the essays. Alex has gifted the industry with his 'Flight and Flying' collections, which are an excellent read for professionals and students alike."

Dr. Suzanne Kearns
Assistant Professor, Commercial Aviation Management
DAN Management and Organizational Studies
Western University

FLIGHT AND FLYING

Volume 1

A collection of essays on the
art and science of flight and flying

Alex Burton BA, MSc, ATPL
Cover and photography Stella Giacomazzi

International Standard Book Number 13: 978-1-60452-096-5
International Standard Book Number 10: 1-60452-096-5
Library of Congress Control Number: 2014945839

BluewaterPress LLC
52 Tuscan Way Ste 202-309
Saint Augustine Florida 32092

http://www.bluewaterpress.com

This book may be purchased online at -
http://www.bluewaterpress.com/flyingv1

Printed in the United States of America

Dedication

This collection is dedicated to all those who shared their wisdom and experience with me, to those with whom I shared this adventure we call the miracle of flight, and to my wife, the most patient and forgiving person with whom I share all my adventures and without whom none of this would be possible.

And, to my long time mentor and friend,

Jan Herman Spronk, Major RNLAF (Ret.),
May 13, 1926 – June 15, 2014.

May he find only warm tailwinds to carry him onward.

INTRODUCTION

"I think it is a pity to lose the romantic side of flying and simply to accept it as a common means of transport...."

-Amy Johnson

Flight and flying captured me from my early days. As a child I built hot air balloons, balsa gliders, models, and free flight balsa and paper powered machines. Both my father and my uncle had been pilots during WWII. My dad learned powered flight on the Aeronca C-3, a 36 hp flying machine launched with a cable tethered to a pole attached to the left wing tip, much like a tether ball kids play in the school yard. The pilot released the plane from the tether once it had achieved flying speed, about 30 MPH. Budd Davisson describes the C-3 as an, "...almost-airplane whose chromosomes are heavily tainted by an ancestor's illicit love affair with a box kite."

My dad went on to fly the B-25, which, I expect, was an improvement over the C-3. Both my dad and my uncle returned to "normal" life following the war, working as aerospace engineers.

My career has been, for the most part, involved with teaching and exploring the process of learning and understanding. As a flight instructor and pilot examiner, working with people on their path toward recreational flying or careers in aviation has been a pleasure: enjoyable and very satisfying. Writing and speaking on various aspects of flight and flying have, naturally, become a part of that process.

This collection of essays was written over a period of several years, and each of the essays was published in one or more aviation journals including the COPA Journal, the Aviation News Journal, Mentor Magazine, and online on the International Association of Flight Training Professionals website. The articles touch aspects of a variety of topics including theory of flight, flight operations, manoeuvres, takeoffs and landings, navigation, flight instruction, human factors, and aviation safety.

Volume 1 of Flight and Flying focuses on the Theory of Flight, Flight Manoeuvres, Flight Instruction, Human Factors, and Aviation Safety. Volume 2 focuses on Flight Operations, Takeoff and Landing Considerations, and Navigation.

Each essay stands alone. Each was written at a particular time and place and was a reflection of a problem or topic that was of interest to me at that particular time.

In some ways, the writing of each piece was a way for me, personally, to foster my own clarity on the topic and provide an opportunity to investigate the topic in more depth than I might otherwise have done. As Mark Twain wrote, "A man who carries a cat by the tail learns something he can learn in no other way." Such was my process.

The essays are loosely organized under general headings for convenience. I encourage the reader to pick and choose particular pieces in any order or sequence that seems most interesting or helpful to his or her own process at a given moment.

This collection is not intended to be a comprehensive text on aviation. I make no claim to be an expert or to provide the last word on any topic. I write mostly for my own enjoyment and as a way to explore, to sound out thoughts and ideas I found of interest at a particular moment in time, either professionally or personally.

Learning is an ongoing life long process. Writing, for me, is one way to continue that exploration and learning process.

Enjoy.

Alex Burton BA, MSc, ATPL
Abbotsford, BC

Contents

PART 1: THEORY OF FLIGHT

Chapter 1.1

Centre of Gravity

"The best and safest thing is to keep a balance in your life, acknowledge the great powers around us and in us. If you can do that, and live that way, you are really a wise man."

-Euripides, 484 BC – 406 BC

Some time back I received a note from a young pilot. He wrote, "I remember reading Lindbergh loaded the Spirit of St. Louis with an excessively aft centre of gravity for his trip across the Atlantic. I vaguely remember the reason was that the aircraft would have to be trimmed well forward to compensate, and that this would derive more lift from the stabilizer in the rear giving more total lift and hence more efficiency. What's the reasoning behind this? Is it true?"

I haven't read the original document Evan writes about, but the reasoning seems sound to me. An aft *centre of gravity* certainly does give an aircraft an advantage in the area of endurance and fuel economy. It does, however, also result in some disadvantages.

Like life, aircraft loading is a series of compromises. If we understand the trade-offs, we can make our decisions based on knowledge and understanding and load our aircraft to optimize for the characteristics most important on a particular flight.

The force we refer to as lift, produced by the wings, holds an aircraft aloft. For an aircraft to remain in level flight, lift produced by the wings must equal the machine's weight. We refer to this condition as equilibrium. If lift exceeds weight, the aircraft will accelerate vertically in proportion to the weight/lift differential; if weight exceeds lift, the aircraft will accelerate vertically downwards also in proportion to the differential.

The average of the lift force produced by the wing or aerofoil acts through the point we refer to as the *centre of pressure* and at right angles to the wing's chord line. Weight acts through the point we refer to as the *centre of gravity* in a direct line from the *centre of gravity* of the aircraft to the centre of gravity of the earth, regardless of the aircraft's attitude.

A design feature of most aircraft is to position the *centre of pressure* during normal flight conditions aft of the *centre of gravity*, creating a dynamic tension or torque between the two forces of lift and weight. This ensures the aircraft will have a designed-in tendency to put its nose down in the event lift is lost or significantly reduced, for example in a stall. This is a useful and life-preserving tendency, one we don't want to give up lightly.

We achieve stability in aircraft not through equal directly opposed forces but through the balance of eccentric forces, forces that are intentionally designed to act in dynamic tension. When forces act opposite and parallel to one another we refer to them as a couple. Lift and weight are a couple. Thrust and drag are also a couple.

To balance two opposing eccentric forces a third force is needed. In this case, we depend on the force produced by the horizontal stabilizer or stabilator to balance the torque resulting from offsetting the forces of lift and weight.

The horizontal stabilizer, normally found at the tail of an aircraft, is an aerofoil much like the wing except it produces negative lift, lift directed downward under normal flight conditions rather than upward. Its work is to push the tail section of the aircraft downward to counteract the tendency of the wing to lift the tail up and over the *centre of gravity*. Quite simple. Quite elegant.

When teaching this concept, I find many students can make good use of the image of a mobile. Imagine a stick suspended by a string. We'll think of that string as the force resulting from lift: its pull is upward. A weight is suspended from the stick just to one side of the attachment point of the string: its pull is downward. We can think of this weight as the *centre of gravity*. At some distance on the other side of the string's attach point a much smaller weight is suspended to counterbalance the tendency of the first weight to pull the stick out of horizontal. We can imagine this weight as the tail-force working to keep the stick level.

Or, we might imagine a teeter-totter. An adult can successfully teeter-totter with a young child simply by sitting close to the balance point. Remember, force is equal to mass multiplied by distance (F = m x d).

What we must achieve, if we are to successfully fly an aircraft in level flight, is a working balance among the three forces: lift, produced by the wings; weight, the mass of the aircraft; and tail force, the downward force produced by the negative lift of the tail plane so the aircraft can remain in a level attitude.

Now we come to the question of moving the *centre of gravity* forward or aft within the limits established and published by the aircraft manufacturer. The *centre of pressure* essentially remains stationary while the wing is in a normal flight attitude.

The farther forward we move the *centre of gravity* the more we increase the aircraft's tendency to put its nose down. To keep the aircraft in a level flying attitude, it becomes necessary to increase the amount of down-force the stabilizer or stabilator produces. Normally, we do this by trimming, adjusting the angle at which the aerofoil meets the relative airflow.

We do, however, produce some measurable changes in the aircraft's performance characteristics as we move the *centre of gravity* forward and make the necessary adjustments to compensate for the change.

The increased down-force required from the tail section to maintain longitudinal balance acts on the aircraft *as if it were increased weight*. Effectively, as the *centre of gravity* is moved forward the aircraft becomes heavier. The wing must now produce sufficient lift to equal both the weight of the aircraft and the amount of down force produced by the stabilizer.

A heavier aircraft experiences increased wing loading and requires additional lift to maintain level flight. To produce additional lift, we must either increase air speed or increase angle of attack. An increase in angle of attack reduces our margin from the critical angle of attack — the stall — and thus increases our stall speed. It also produces additional induced drag. Additional drag requires additional thrust. Additional thrust requires increased fuel burn.

An excessively forward *centre of gravity* might reduce elevator control authority, required to lift the nose at low airspeed, for example on take-off or landing. An excessively forward *centre of gravity* might result in insufficient elevator authority to produce a nose up attitude at normal approach and landing speeds.

There is some good news, however. An aircraft with a more forward *centre of gravity* is a more stable aircraft. It will be much quicker to recover from a stall or the condition of approaching stall, and, being heavier, it will have a higher manoeuvring speed. It will have the ability to safely fly faster in turbulent conditions. Moving the *centre of gravity* forward also increases the arm between the aircraft's point of rotation, the *centre of gravity*, and the rudder and elevator, increasing the power of those flight control surfaces.

As the *centre of gravity* is moved forward, the positive control responses of the elevator and rudder increase, enhancing manoeuvrability.

The other side of the story is essentially the reverse. An aircraft with a more aft *centre of gravity* will require less down tail-force to balance the decreased distance — reduced torque — between the *centre of gravity* and the *centre of pressure*. It will have a lower stall speed due to its reduced weight, angle of attack, and wing loading. Endurance and range increase; induced drag is reduced. The thrust required to produce a given airspeed will be less than that required for the same aircraft in a heavier configuration.

The negative side of the equation, in extreme situations, is that, should the aircraft stall, it may become extremely difficult or impossible to achieve recovery. The nose will not come down: an entirely unsatisfactory condition. The effectiveness of the rudder and elevators will also be reduced.

So, Lindbergh was certainly on the right track by loading his aircraft with a rear *centre of gravity*. For him, the critical factor for success on his flight across the Atlantic was to ensure maximum range with available fuel. The North Atlantic Ocean would certainly be a poor landing site for a small aircraft.

By loading the Spirit of St. Lewis with a rearward *centre of gravity*, Lindbergh would have established a situation to maximize his range. His aircraft would be able to fly with the least possible *angle of attack* (minimum induced drag), the lowest possible wing loading and down tail-force (minimum weight), and would require the least amount of thrust (power) for a given airspeed.

Knowing how to correctly load your aircraft for a particular flight can enable you, too, to maximize its performance for that particular flight.

If you are anticipating turbulence, perhaps during a trip through the mountains, or if you intend to practice spins and other aerobatic manoeuvres, a more forward *centre of gravity* loading would be the preferred choice. If you require maximum range, power efficiency, do not intend to do any complex manoeuvring, or if you expect reasonably calm conditions a more aft *centre of gravity* would be a better fit.

Understanding how the forces at work on your aircraft in flight can enable you to make positive informed decisions on how to maximize its performance for the conditions you intend to face. Of course, we must always ensure that whatever variation on our loading we choose, we take off with the *centre of gravity* within the published limits for the aircraft.

NOTES:

Chapter 1.2

Effect of Weight on Aircraft Performance

"Gravity never loses. The best you can hope for is a draw."

-Aviation 101

Preparing for a flight? Completion of a weight and balance calculation is an essential and required part of the process.

For commercial flights and other "formal" occasions, for example your flight-test or check ride, the weight and balance procedure will be written out and detailed. For casual recreational flights, the process may be a bit less formal, but we are still legally responsible to ensure our aircraft is within limits, both in terms of overall weight and C of G position.

The weight and centre of gravity of an aircraft are important for the entire duration of a flight, not just at take-off. Many aircraft, particularly aircraft with complex fuel systems, are capable of both changing their weight as a result of fuel burn and moving their C of G.

Many aircraft are able to take off at a weight well in excess of their maximum landing weight. Even light aircraft, the newer C-182s as one example has a maximum take-off weight of 3100 lbs. Its maximum landing weight is 2950 lbs.

Leaving the C of G problem for another day, let's take a look at weight. Weight is a factor in all aspects of aircraft performance. Stall speed, maximum range airspeed, maximum endurance airspeed, maximum distance and minimum sink glide speeds, takeoff roll and landing distance, rate of climb, and manoeuvring speed are all examples of aircraft performance tied directly to aircraft weight.

Back in ground school we learned about the four forces involved in aircraft flight: lift, weight, thrust, and drag. Thrust opposes drag. Lift opposes weight. We say that these forces act as couples.

If opposing forces are equal, for example if thrust equals drag and lift equals weight, we say the aircraft is in a state of equilibrium; aircraft performance will remain constant. However, if lift exceeds weight, the opposing forces of lift and weight are no longer equal. The aircraft is no longer in equilibrium and a change in flight performance will occur. In this case, when lift exceeds weight, the aircraft will accelerate vertically.

If we can put some numbers to formulas for a couple of specific examples without getting lost in the mathematics, it makes it very easy to see the relationship between aircraft weight and performance. Let's take a look at the stall and at rate of climb.

First, the stall:

The formula for lift, which we all remember from ground school, is: **Lift = ½($C_L SpV^2$).** The formula tells us that lift is equal to one-half the product of four factors:

1. The Angle of Attack. Increasing the angle of attack increases the amount of lift and reaches its maximum value at the Critical Angle of Attack. Increasing the angle of attack beyond the critical angle of attack results in a significant reduction of lift: a stall. The point at which the stall is reached depends on the shape of the wing profile and the angle of attack at which it is being flown. This is expressed in the formula for lift by the Coefficient of Lift (CL); the critical angle of attack, the angle at which maximum lift is produced, is represented as CLmax.

2. The Square of the Airspeed (V^2). Increasing airspeed results in a significant increase in lift. We can see from the formula that lift increases with the Square of the Velocity. If we double the airspeed we increase lift four fold.

3. Air Density (p). Density decreases with altitude and increased temperature. Lower density results in less lift.

4. Wing Surface (S). Larger wing surfaces produce more lift.

For our purposes, we can say C_L, **S** and p remain constant. Once our aircraft is in flight at a given altitude we can make the assumption that the surface area of our wings, barring some tragic occurrence, and the air density will remain constant. Since we are speaking of the stall, which occurs at a fixed angle of attack, we can consider C_L as a constant using the value for C_{Lmax}.

To simplify our lives as we look at the issue of weight, we can assign the product of the factors for C_L, **S** and p in the formula for lift a constant value, let's say "*K*". So we can look at our formula, in its simplified form, as **Lift = KV²**: lift is equal to *K* times the square of the velocity.

Let's use a typical training aircraft which most of us have flown at one point or another for numbers: the C-172. According to the POH for the 1976 M model, the stall speed, depending on the position of the centre of gravity, is approximately 50 KCAS at gross weight, 2300 lbs. This gives us some numbers to work with.

Reminding ourselves that in un-accelerated flight lift is equal to weight, we can say that weight is also equal to our constant "**K**" times the square of the velocity (**W = KV²**).

If we plug in our numbers and solve for **K**, we can apply that number using weights other than full gross. **V** = 50 KCAS (from the POH); **W** = 2300 lbs. Using the formula we see that 2300 = **K** x 2500 or we could express this as **K** = 2300/2500. Solving for **K** we find, in this case, **K** = 0.92.

Let's see what happens to the stall speed when we reduce the weight to, say, 1800 lbs., a reduction of 500 lbs., 22% of our gross weight. Now, **V²** =1800/0.92. In this case we find our 1g-stall speed at 1800 lbs. would be 44.2 KCAS, a 12% reduction in the stall speed.

A rule of thumb suggested by William Kershner[1] for finding the effects of weight change on airspeed is to, "…reduce the airspeed by one-half of the percentage of the Weight reduction". In this case that would give us a "rule of thumb" stall speed of approximately 44.5 KCAS. It isn't quite as precise, perhaps, but it certainly is in the ballpark.

I don't know about your eyes, but I would certainly have a difficult time finding the difference on the airspeed indicator between 44.2 and 44.5.

Rate of climb is another performance factor dependent on the flying weight of the aircraft. Rate of climb is a function of two factors: excess thrust horsepower and weight. It is generally expressed by the formula: Rate of Climb is equal to Excess Thrust Horse Power times 33,000 divided by Weight (**R/C=ETHP x 33,000/W**).[2]

33,000 (550 x 60) is simply the conversion of horsepower, which is normally expressed in foot-pounds per second, into foot-pounds per minute.[3] We normally measure rate of climb in terms of feet per minute, so it reduces confusion to keep our units consistent. I don't know about you, but I certainly have a sufficiency of confusion in my life, already.

Going back to our C-172 POH, we find, under standard conditions at gross weight, Cessna tells us we can expect a rate of climb of 645'/min at sea level. Plugging this information into our formula for Rate of Climb we find that the aircraft produces approximately 45 Excess Thrust Horse Power (645 = 45 x 33,000/2300) under these conditions.

If we reduce our weight to 1800 lbs. and again run the formula, assuming the same excess thrust horse power—this is simplifying just a bit, but it demonstrates the point—we find that the Rate of Climb has increased to 825'/minute, a 128% increase (R/C = 45 x 33,000/1800).

The teacher in me wants to say here, "So, what can we learn from this?" On a practical day-to-day level: increased weight equals increase stall speed; decreased weight equals increase rate of climb, and vice versa. If we need to get more specific, we can always do the math.

A nice rule of thumb for most light aircraft is that a 10% increase in take-off weight will result in a 5% increase in take-off speed, at least a 9% decrease in acceleration, and at least a 21% increase in take-off distance.[4]

We've all been tempted at one time or another to have a go at a short runway possibly with an obstacle at the end when loaded just a little on the heavy side. What a perfect moment to remember: the numbers don't lie.

All considered it's a healthy concept to keep in mind: the flying weight of your aircraft directly affects its performance. Each time. Every time. No exceptions.

NOTES:

Chapter 1.3

Density Altitude and Summer Flying

"Louisiana in September was like an obscene phone call from nature. The air - moist, sultry, secretive, and far from fresh - felt as if it were being exhaled into one's face. Sometimes it even sounded like heavy breathing."

-Tom Robbins

Here we are looking squarely at summer: June, July and August. It's a beautiful day. What say we get a few friends together and go for a burn? An excellent idea as long as we remember beautiful warm days can hide some potentially dangerous situations if we are not informed and prepared.

Looking through accident reports from the past several years for a particular time of year can reveal some interesting and instructive information. We hear lots of stories about the dangers of ice and snow and freezing in winter, but what are some of the hazards of this time of year that have led pilots in Canada to grief? One of the items that appear in too many accident reports as a contributing factor is Density Altitude.

Let's take a look.

On June 8, 1997, a Piper J4A in the initial climb after take-off from Ponsonby, Ontario, was observed by witnesses to bank steeply to the right, pitch nose-down, and strike the ground. The pilot was fatally injured; the passenger later died of his injuries. The aircraft was destroyed by fire.

Findings:

- The high gross weight of the aircraft resulted in reduced aircraft climb performance.
- The aircraft stalled, for undetermined reasons, at too low an altitude to be recovered.

On August 3, 1997, a Cessna 337 on fire patrol out of Nelson, BC, flew low up a valley, commenced a steep, left turn and crashed into the mountainside. The aircraft was destroyed at impact; the two occupants were fatally injured.

Findings:

- The combination of high air temperature and altitude reduced aircraft climb performance.
- When the pilot entered a steep turn to avoid the rising terrain, the stall speed increased; as a result, the aircraft stalled.

On June 13, 2000, a Cessna 180E, about five miles north-west of Campbell River, BC, over McIvor Lake, entered a left-hand, steeply banked climbing turn. During the turn, the aircraft's nose dropped abruptly and the aircraft descended to strike the shoreline in a near-vertical, slightly left-wing-low attitude. The three occupants died on impact. The aircraft sustained substantial damage.

Findings:

- The pilot, while manoeuvring the aircraft, induced an aerodynamic stall.
- The heavy weight of the aircraft increased the risk of a stall.
- The initiation of a low-speed climbing turn increased the risk of a stall.

On July 1, 2000, an Aeronca 65-CA attempted to avoid trees at the end of the runway at Fort Steele, BC. As it approached the trees, its bank angle appeared steep, and the aircraft pitched nose down, descended rapidly, and struck a house. The pilot and passenger were seriously injured. The aircraft was substantially damaged.

Findings:

- The aircraft was close to its maximum gross take-off weight and had degraded performance because of the relatively high density altitude. As a result, the angle of climb was too shallow to clear the trees at the end of the airstrip.
- The pilot's attempt to manoeuvre to avoid the trees resulted in a stall at an altitude that was too low for the pilot to recover.

Pulling the threads of these accidents together leads us to some important safety considerations for flying in the warm summer months. In each of these accidents, the pilots were qualified for the intended flight and there appeared to be no mechanical problems with any of the aircraft prior to their contact with the ground. All of the aircraft were at or approaching their gross weight, and temperatures were above standard, in the 20 to 30 degree Celsius range. In the case of the 180E, no information is given regarding temperature, but the accident occurred on 13 June, and the weather included light rain and mist. Humidity, along with altitude and temperature, is a factor that increases density altitude.

In ground school, we generally discuss in one form or another, the concept of the "4 Hs": high, heavy, hot, and humid, also known as altitude, aircraft weight, outside air temperature, and relative humidity. Each of these is a factor affecting aircraft performance.

Manoeuvring an aircraft increases G loading, increasing wing loading and stall speed just to put icing on the cake.

Our "ideal" scenario for aircraft operation would be low altitude, a light load, and a cold dry day.

In each of the accidents described above, at least three of the four Hs were on the wrong side of pretty, and the pilots were manoeuvring just prior to the stall and subsequent crash.

One of the key windows we have for predicting reduction in aircraft performance is to understand the concept of density altitude. We all learned how to calculate density altitude back in ground school and probably retained that information right through the written exam. Understanding how the concept relates to aircraft performance and making the needed allowances for the effect it has might just save your life.

In simple terms, density altitude is pressure altitude corrected for temperature. It gives us what I like to think of as the aircraft's *experiential altitude* or *performance altitude*, the altitude at which the aircraft "thinks" it's flying. Let's work through an example.

Pressure altitude is easy enough. We just set our altimeter to 29.92, standard pressure, and read pressure altitude off the dial. Or, if we know the altimeter setting from listening to an ATIS broadcast, we can take our station pressure – the altimeter setting we get off the ATIS broadcast – and subtract that from 29.92. We know that 1" Hg is equivalent to 1000' in altitude; a higher than standard station pressure will indicate a lower pressure altitude and a lower than standard station pressure will indicate a higher pressure altitude.

In terms of performance, "High station pressure: happy. Low station pressure: head's up."

Let's say the station pressure, our altimeter reading, is 29.02" Hg. We take standard pressure, 29.92, and subtract our station pressure, 29.02, getting a difference of +0.90, +900'. Remember that 1" Hg is equivalent to 1000' of altitude (+0.90 x 1000 = +900). The pressure drops as we increase altitude so we know that our pressure altitude will be 900' higher than our station altitude. If our aerodrome altitude is, for example, 1800', our pressure altitude on the ground is 2700' (1800' + 900').

With this information and the outside air temperature (OAT), we can go directly to a handy Koch Chart. You can find a copy of the chart in your Canadian Flight Supplement, Section C, Planning. The Koch Chart gives us a quick generic reference for determining performance degradation in relation to pressure altitude and temperature, which is another way of saying density altitude. It basically does the density altitude calculations for us.

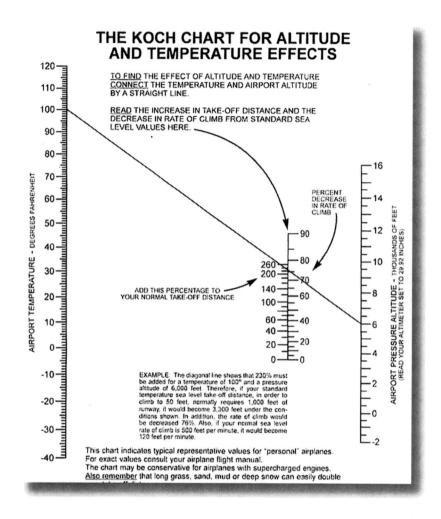

THE KOCH CHART FOR ALTITUDE AND TEMPERATURE EFFECTS

TO FIND THE EFFECT OF ALTITUDE AND TEMPERATURE CONNECT THE TEMPERATURE AND AIRPORT ALTITUDE BY A STRAIGHT LINE.

READ THE INCREASE IN TAKE-OFF DISTANCE AND THE DECREASE IN RATE OF CLIMB FROM STANDARD SEA LEVEL VALUES HERE.

PERCENT DECREASE IN RATE OF CLIMB

ADD THIS PERCENTAGE TO YOUR NORMAL TAKE-OFF DISTANCE

AIRPORT TEMPERATURE - DEGREES FAHRENHEIT

AIRPORT PRESSURE ALTITUDE - THOUSANDS OF FEET (READ YOUR ALTIMETER SET TO 29.92 INCHES)

EXAMPLE: The diagonal line shows that 230% must be added for a temperature of 100° and a pressure altitude of 6,000 feet. Therefore, if your standard temperature sea level take-off distance, in order to climb to 50 feet, normally requires 1,000 feet of runway, it would become 3,300 feet under the conditions shown. In addition, the rate of climb would be decreased 76%. Also, if your normal sea level rate of climb is 500 feet per minute, it would become 120 feet per minute.

This chart indicates typical representative values for "personal" airplanes. For exact values consult your airplane flight manual. The chart may be conservative for airplanes with supercharged engines. Also remember that long grass, sand, mud or deep snow can easily double

In our example, we determined our station's pressure altitude is 2700'.

Let's give ourselves an OAT of 30⁰ C, just to make things interesting. If we draw a line on the Koch Chart connecting those two points — 2700' and 30⁰ — we see we can expect a decrease in rate of climb of approximately 50% and an increase in ground roll of approximately 80%.

If a C-172 at gross weight, for example, will require an 865' ground roll at standard temperature and pressure at sea level, we can expect, under the conditions we have chosen for our example, a ground roll of 1557'. If our normal SL rate of climb is 680'/min, in our example scenario we can expect a rate of climb of only 340'/min. These are not numbers that would encourage a prudent pilot to launch off a short runway with trees at the end unless he or she did some careful calculations to ensure a safe take-off was certain.

If we want to be a bit more specific, we can determine the density altitude ourselves and work from there. Using our E-6B flight computer we look in the window for True Airspeed & Density Altitude, set the air temperature over the pressure altitude and read the density altitude. Or, for those who have one, a CX-2 flight computer will do all the work for us and produce a very accurate answer.

In this example we read a density altitude of approximately 5000'. Getting back to our example, this means that although our aerodrome has an altitude of 1800' ASL, our aircraft "thinks" and, more importantly, behaves as if it were operating at 5000' ASL.

If we want to find more specific numbers for our particular aircraft rather than use the generic data from the Koch Chart, we can go to the POH and work out the numbers for rate of climb and take-off roll. Comparing sea level figures to our example scenario, my quick calculations show, for a Cherokee Warrior, PA-28-151, the rate of climb will be reduced by 34% and the take-off roll will be increased by 79%.

Aircraft weight can significantly affect aircraft performance. The basic calculation for determining the loading factor is (present weight/max certified weight)^2. If we go back to our example C-172 aircraft with a gross weight 2300 lbs., which had a 865' ground roll at gross weight at sea level, and reduce its weight by, say, 20% to 1840 lbs., we determine that its take-off roll will be reduced to 553' [(1840/2300)^2 x 865 = 553'. Take a look in your own aircraft's POH, if it has the numbers for various take-off weights, and see what a difference a few pounds can make.

We mentioned humidity earlier, and I don't want to just let it get by without a wee bit more detail. While humidity is not nearly as significant a factor as temperature, pressure, or weight it does have adverse effects on aircraft performance. Given two masses of air with the same temperature, the moist air mass will always be less dense.

Water vapour in the air affects both engine power output, with piston engines, and the amount of lift an aerofoil can produce. High humidity, in effect, increases the density altitude by decreasing the ambient air density. In extreme conditions with high humidity combined with high temperature, a piston engine aircraft may experience as much as a 12% reduction in power output. Your 250-hp engine is now putting out 220 hp.

What all these calculations demonstrate for us, without getting lost in the particular numbers, is that heat, altitude, weight, and humidity can seriously degrade aircraft performance. In high density altitude conditions, our take-off roll will be extended, our rate of climb will be reduced, and our aircraft's ability to manoeuvre will be impaired. As pilots responsible for ensuring safe flight, what we need to know and understand about these factors is the specific ways they will affect the aircraft we are intending to fly.

A hot day does not cause an accident. Neither does operating an aircraft at gross weight or in a light drizzle or taking-off from an aerodrome with a high density altitude. However, coupling these factors with a serious underestimation of their effects on performance and a pilot who thinks he or she can manoeuvre an aircraft in the same manner and expect the same performance as at sea level on a normal day can set the stage for a tragic outcome.

Just as we know visibility, turbulence, and icing are factors that must be considered before commencing flight, so too are heat, altitude, weight, and humidity. Knowing what to expect from an aircraft under any particular flight conditions allows us to make the decisions that will result in a safe and enjoyable flight.

NOTES:

Chapter 1.4

Density Altitude Formula[5]

Just for fun, here is another way to calculate density altitude that is, perhaps, worth putting into your bag of tricks. We can use the formula:

Density Altitude = Pressure Altitude + (120 x ΔT)

Where ΔT = difference between the actual temperature at a given station or altitude and ISA standard. ΔT may be positive or negative.

Example, picking a hot day at an airport with relatively high elevation:

Airport elevation at Calgary/Springbank (CYBW) = **3940'**
Altimeter setting = **28.86" Hg**
Temperature = **+31⁰C**

Pressure Altitude @ CYBW = Standard (29.92) – Station (28.86) x 1000 + station altitude
PA = (29.92 – 28.86) x 1000 + 3940
PA = 1.06 x 1000 + 3940' = **5000'**

ISA standard air temperature at station = 15 – 1.98(station altitude/1000) = **7.8⁰C**

ΔT = Actual air temperature – ISA Standard air temperature

ΔT = 31 – 7.8 = **23.2⁰C**

Density Altitude @ CYBW on our sample day:

DA = PA + (120 x ΔT) →

DA = 5000 + (120 x 23.2) = 7784'

On this sample day, the aeroplane will perform as if it were flying at 7784' ASL.

Chapter 1.5

Manoeuvring Speed (Va)

"Any fool can carry on but a wise man knows how to shorten sail in time."

-Joseph Conrad

Turbulence is something we all experience at one time or another. In ground school we learned the theoretical explanation: turbulence is an irregular movement of air resulting from eddies and vertical currents; it is produced under four types of conditions.

Mechanical turbulence is produced when air passes over the ground, particularly irregular ground, and manmade objects. Thermal turbulence is a result of differential ground heating. Frontal turbulence is produced along the interface of moving air masses, and wind shear, a shift in wind direction or velocity at altitude, can also produce significant turbulence.

Regardless the source of turbulence, the experience of pilots, passengers, and the aircraft itself are the same. Depending on the severity of the turbulence, we can expect all the delights of discomfort, airsickness, possible injury, and, in severe cases, potential loss of control or structural damage to the aircraft.

It is important to understand the causes of turbulence, to learn to recognize situations that may be difficult or hazardous, and to understand the limitations and procedures to ensure safe flight in your aircraft. Two important items on our list of things to know and understand are the load limits of the particular aircraft we are flying and our aircraft's manoeuvring speed, V_a[6]

As a friend of mine asked, "Isn't V_a just a number in the POH?"

The answer is to that is, of course, yes it is. But there is also more, if you are interested.

The POH for the aircraft you fly will provide specific information regarding load limits. The vast majority of aircraft flying with a Certificate of Airworthiness (C of A) are classified in either **Normal** or **Utility** category. In order to hold a C of A in the **Normal** category, an aircraft must be able to safely withstand a load of +3.8g and –1.52g. **Utility** category aircraft must safely withstand a load of +4.4g and –1.76g. These are the legally established minimums.[7]

Some aircraft may be flown in either category, the C-172, for example, depending on how it is loaded with passengers, baggage, and fuel.

Most aircraft are designed to exceed these minimums. If we look in the POH for our 1976 Cessna 172M, for example, we see the aircraft meets or exceeds the minimum requirements and is designed to have a 50% "safety factor" above and beyond the minimums. This "safety factor" would define the "ultimate load factor". When this limit is exceeded, parts of the aircraft's primary structure, i.e. wings, empennage, or engine may begin to depart company. It is important to note, in the case of Cessna, the design load factor limit drops to +3.0 with flaps extended. The POH does not give information regarding load limits for negative gs with flaps deployed, but we do note that the negative g load limit is considerably less than that given and required for positive loading.

This means, in the case of our C-172, we can impose a load with flaps up of +3.8g, or –1.52g with the aircraft loaded in accordance with **Normal Category** specifications without damaging the aircraft. Applying a slightly greater load to the aircraft will not immediately result in the loss of vital surfaces or components due to the built-in safety factor. However, we all know the story about old pilots and bold pilots. If we continue to knock on a door, eventually someone will answer. The over-stress your aircraft door is not a great one on which to continue knocking.

Knowingly stressing an aircraft above its limits can lead to serious and possibly fatal consequences down the line, if not sooner.

A "g" is a measure of acceleration. When we are speaking about aircraft we normally measure g loads in terms of the lift to weight ratio (L/W). In normal, un-accelerated flight we experience a 1g load: the lift produced by the aerofoils is equal to the weight of the aircraft, including any tail loading being produced. We can say, under these conditions, that the **load factor**, the ratio between the **dead load**, the weight of the aircraft, and the **live load,** any increased weight of the aircraft caused by acceleration, is 1.

If we change our aircraft's attitude -- apply control inputs -- bank the aircraft or initiate a climb or any other manoeuvre, we produce acceleration as a natural outcome of changing the aircraft's flight path. The more rapidly or aggressively we change the aircraft's flight path the greater the acceleration.

Acceleration increases the live load.

Increasing the live load increases the load factor. The greater the acceleration we produce -- the greater the difference between lift and weight -- the greater the load on the aircraft. We can think of acceleration loading as the difference between the amount of lift required to hold the aircraft in level un-accelerated flight and the additional lift we have created by control inputs causing change in the aircraft's flight path.

The formula for lift, which we all remember from ground school, is: **Lift = 1/2C$_L$SpV^2.** The formula tells us that lift is equal to one-half the product of four factors:

The **Angle of Attack.** Increasing the angle of attack increases the amount of lift and reaches its maximum value at the **Critical Angle of Attack.** Increasing the angle of attack beyond the critical angle of attack results in a significant reduction of lift: a stall. The point at which the stall is reached depends on the shape of the wing profile and the angle of attack. This is expressed in the formula for lift by the **Coefficient of Lift (C$_L$);** the critical angle of attack, the angle at which maximum lift is produced, is represented as C$_{Lmax}$.

The **Square of the Airspeed (V^2).** Increasing airspeed results in an increase in lift. We can see from the formula that lift increases with the Square of the Velocity. If we double the airspeed, we increase lift four fold.

Air Density (p). Density decreases with altitude and increased temperature. Lower density results in less lift.

Wing Surface (S). Larger wing surfaces produce more lift.

For our purposes, we can assume that the **C$_L$, S** and **p** remain constant. Once our aircraft is loaded and in the air we have little ability to change the coefficient of lift, except as a function of angle of attack, the surface area of our wings, or the air density. To simplify our lives we can assign their product in the formula for lift a constant value, let's say "K". So we can look at our formula, in its simplified form, as **Lift = KV^2.** Lift is equal to K times the square of the velocity.

This lets us see a bit more clearly the relationship between lift and air speed. Lift increases with the square of the air speed. Let's go back aboard the C-172 and see how this works.

If we slow the 172 down to just at stall speed, flying at our maximum angle of attack, C$_{Lmax}$, and pull the control column full back, the aircraft will stall; we, and the aircraft, will experience a 1g load. The wings are incapable of producing more than 1 g at that speed. If we pull our control column full back while flying at a higher speed and smaller angle of attack, we will produce more than a 1g load; at the moment of stall we will be accelerating.

For the sake of simplicity, let's say the aircraft will perform a 1g stall at 50 knots (flaps up). As we just discussed, the load applied to our aircraft is increased by the square of the speed. If we increase our speed to say 1.41 times the stall speed, 70.5 knots, and apply full elevator input to stall the aircraft, we find we experience a 2g load (1.41 x 1.41 = 2).

If we were to double the speed at which we stall the aircraft, say from 50 knots to 100 knots, we increase the load by four times (4 being the square of 2). If we apply full control inputs at 100 knots and stall the aircraft, instead of the mild, rather pleasant 1g stall, the aircraft and we will experience a 4g dose of acceleration. This could well pose a problem if our aircraft is operating in the normal category and is rated to accept a +3.8g load.

How do we determine the maximum speed at which we can safely apply full control inputs without exceeding our load limits? We work backwards from the correct answer.

Without beating the math to death, we remember that a 45° bank turn produces a 1.41g loading; a 60° bank turn produces a 2g loading. We can look these values up and save ourselves some effort, or we can work them out. We can derive them either mathematically or geometrically. Mathematically, we find that $G = 1/\cos \theta$. θ is the angle of bank in degrees.

One divided by the cosine of our angle of bank is the multiplier of our weight to find live load or "G" force. For example, the $\cos 60° = 0.5$; $1/\cos 60° = 2.0$. Geometrically we can draw the triangles representing vertical and horizontal lift, measure the lengths of the sides, and work out the ratio between lift and weight. While we are speaking here about turns, any change in an aircraft's flight path-- up, down, or sideways--will result in acceleration.

If we go back to our formula for Lift, using our simplified version (Lift = KV^2), remembering that at the moment of stall Weight is equal to Lift, we can say that Weight = KV^2). From this, we can find the relationship between Lift and Velocity by solving for V: $V = \sqrt{W/K}$.

Stall speed increases with the square root of the load factor.

For example, if our aircraft normally stalls at 50 knots in level un-accelerated flight, in a 45° bank turn we can expect a stall speed of 59.4 Knots (50 x √1.41). In a 60° bank turn we can expect a stall speed of 70.7 (50 x √2).

To calculate the maximum stall speed that will keep us on the sunny side of our load factor, we should ask ourselves this question: at what stall speed will lift produce a load factor of 3.8?

Since stall speed increases with the square root of the load factor, we can say the square root of our maximum load factor (3.8) multiplied by the stall speed (V_s): (50 x 1.95 = 97.5) will be our maximum speed. At any airspeed less than Vs times the square root of our maximum load factor, our aircraft will stall before more load is imposed on it than it is designed to handle. The wings cannot produce more load than the aircraft is designed to deal with.

Enter the concept of Manoeuvring Speed (V_a).

As student pilots, we all learn Manoeuvring Speed (V_a); it is one of the three speeds that must be memorized for the Private Pilot flight test. We learn that V_a is the maximum speed [at a particular weight] at which full deflection of the controls can be made without exceeding the design limit load factor and damaging the airplane's primary structure. We also learn that V_a is the maximum recommended speed for turbulent air penetration. This is good information and will perhaps help us earn pass marks on the Private Pilot flight test.

As we grow and develop as pilots, we begin to take on new challenges. Developing a deeper understanding of V_a becomes essential, particularly if we start thinking about doing any mountain flying or extending our range to distant points from which we will not be able to immediately "return to base" if the weather begins to deteriorate.

The bottom line: V_a is the speed below which our aircraft will stall rather than bend or break when we impose or have imposed on us — as in the event of a vertical gust — an increased load.

But, as with most things, the devil is in the details. If we go back to the POH for our 172, we read that the Manoeuvring speed is given for three weights:

Weight	Va
2300 lbs	98 KCAS
1950 lbs	88 KCAS
1600 lbs	80 KCAS

If we check our POH we see that the actual stall speed at full weight can vary between 50 KCAS and 53 KCAS depending on how forward or aft the C of G is located. This will give us an actual V_a (V_s x √max load factor) of between 97.5 KCAS and 103.4 KIAS at maximum gross weight. Cessna, appropriately, chooses to err on the conservative side in its published figures. As pilots who intend to become old pilots, we should be encouraged to do the same.

Why, we might ask, does V_a decrease with weight? This is an interesting question. As we discussed earlier, the stress or load factor imposed on the aircraft when it is accelerated is a function of the lift to weight ratio. At full weight, 2300 lbs. for our C-172 in the Normal category, we can impose 3.8g, a 3.8 load factor, and remain within safe parameters.

If Lift/Weight = Load Factor, then Lift = Weight x Load Factor. We can generate a total of 8740 lbs. of lift by sudden control input (2300 x 3.8 = 8740) and remain within design limits. The designers of the aircraft have structured the machine to be robust enough to withstand the 3.8 load factor at full weight.

Let's lighten the aircraft and see what happens. If we toss out our passengers and burn off some of the fuel, we might achieve a gross weight of 1600 lbs. At full weight, 2300 lbs., we happily stalled our aircraft at 97.5 KCAS and discovered we experienced 3.8g's (8740/2300 = 3.8). At our new and lighter weight, we can develop the same amount of lift at the same airspeed.

Remember the formula: aircraft weight is not a factor in the production of lift. Unfortunately, when we do the math, we discover that 8740/1600 = 5.5. We've exceeded our load limit by 1.7g's. If we could manage to lighten our aircraft to half its full weight, 1150 lbs., we would find the abrupt stall would now produce a very undesirable 7.6g's (8740/1150 = 7.6). Kids, don't try this at home!

Let's see if we can follow the logic through. The mathematical symbology is clear and simple to those who enjoy the math, but we'll work through it both ways. First, in plain English:

The formula for lift says that lift is equal to the coefficient of lift, multiplied by the surface area of the aircraft's wing, multiplied by half the air density, multiplied by the square of the velocity, $L = 1/2C_L S p V^2$.

Using the simplified version we discussed earlier we can say that $L = K V^2$. We know that a wing stalls just past the angle at which it is providing maximum lift, so we can refer to our CL in terms of its maximum value,

C_{Lmax}. If we make a small jump and say that lift, in a 1g, un-accelerated situation is equal to weight, we see that the aircraft weight is also equal to the coefficient of lift, multiplied by the surface area of the wing, multiplied by half the air density, multiplied by the square of the velocity ($W = KV^2$).

If we take one more step and solve for V (velocity), we see that velocity is equal to the square root of the weight divided by the coefficient of lift, times the surface area, times the air density ($V = \sqrt{W/K}$). If we plug in our known numbers, V = 50 Knots, W = 2300 lbs., we can determine a value for K. In this case it is 0.92 (50x50 = 2300/0.92).

We know from the POH that stall speed at gross weight, depending on the location of the C of G, is approximately 50 KCAS. To calculate the stall speed for a lighter weight, we pop the new weight into our handy little formula. Let's try one with a weight of 1600 lbs. We would say that V^2 = 1600/0.92. In this case we find that our 1g-stall speed at 1600 lbs. would be 41.7 Knots. A rule of thumb suggested by William Kershner for finding the effects of weight change on airspeed is to, "...reduce the airspeed by one-half of the percentage of the Weight reduction". In this case that would give us a "rule of thumb" stall speed of approximately 42.5 Knots. It isn't quite as precise, but it certainly is in the ballpark. I don't know about your eyes, but I would certainly have a difficult time finding the difference on the airspeed indicator between 41.7 and 42.5.

Working back to calculate $\mathbf{V}_a$, remember we multiply the stall speed by the square root of the load factor. In this case: 41.7 x 1.99 = 81.3. Checking our POH chart, we see that Cessna recommends a Va at 1600 lbs. of 80 KCAS.

So, here we are, ready to go flying. Not too many of us are willing to do all the calculations when we are actually flying, especially if the air is a bit turbulent. Nor do we need to do them if we have some reasonable rules of thumb to follow that will keep our passengers and ourselves safe and sound. Here are the rules handed down to me by my mentor, Captain John Spronk[8]:

In **Smooth** flying conditions:

- When flying at least 1000' above the highest obstacle within five miles, use normal cruising speeds.
- When flying lower than 1000', use $\mathbf{V}_a$ (you may need to manoeuvre suddenly)

In **Light** Turbulence:

- Use V_a

In **Moderate** Turbulence:

- Cruising speeds should be reduced to 1.6 - 1.7 x V_s (1.65 is ideal) A speed greater than 1.7 x V_s may result in a speed exceeding V_a in gusts.
- No flaps when flying a Cessna—remember our load factor limit drops to +3.0g's with flaps extended.

In **Severe** Turbulence:

- Slow the aircraft down to 1.5 x Vs. (We need to balance the need to slow down and remain below Va even in gusts while not slowing the aircraft down so much that it may become too difficult to retain control or to where the aircraft stalls with each new gust.)

Once again, no flaps when flying a Cessna.

In the words of General Charles "Chuck" Yeager, "If you want to grow old as a pilot, you've got to know when to push it, and when to back off."

NOTES:

Chapter 1.6

The Climb

"It's wonderful to climb the liquid mountains of the sky. Behind me and before me is God and I have no fears."

-Helen Keller

The essence of an aircraft is that given the correct inputs, it can lift itself off the ground and take to the air. It is a machine that, miraculously, allows us mere humans to move above the surface of our planet in that great sea of air giving us a view of the world enjoyed by only a few fortunate souls.

Without the ability to climb, an aircraft would be merely an expensive bus with parts sticking out making passage through traffic a sore trial.

The ability of an aircraft to climb is termed its climb performance, and there is a great range in climb performance from one aircraft type to another. Some aircraft we think of as having great climb performance. An F-16, for example, according to the Lockheed Martin Corporation, climbs at 50,000 feet per minute at sea level. Some aircraft demonstrate less exciting climb performance. I've watched my little 100 hp Champion Citabria climb out at a blistering rate of 200-300 feet per minute when loaded to gross weight on a warm day.

We rely on our aircraft's climb performance for a number of purposes. Initially, we must move the machine from the ground to the air. We must then be able to clear obstacles in our path, and we must be able to achieve sufficient altitude for a given flight. Perhaps, we might be flying from the coast to an inland destination and, checking our charts, see there are mountains in our way.

Additionally, as altitude increases true airspeed also increases, allowing us to fly faster over the ground and maximize the efficiency of our engine, increasing our range. Reaching an appropriate cruising altitude as soon as possible has considerable advantages.

A number of generic factors affect the ability of any aircraft to climb: the weight of the aircraft, the location of its centre of gravity, density altitude and humidity, use of carburetor heat, deployment of flaps and landing gear, turbulence, and the pilot's accuracy and skill in maintaining correct angle of attack and airspeed.

An aircraft climbs proportionally to excess thrust, total available thrust minus total drag, and inversely in proportion to weight. With propeller driven aircraft, best rate of climb is achieved at the speed that produces maximum excess thrust horsepower (ETHP). ETHP is thrust horsepower produced by the engine/propeller beyond that required to maintain level flight. The aircraft's rate of climb (R/C), how quickly it gains altitude expressed in feet per minute (fpm), can be derived from the formula: R/C = ETHP x 33,000/Weight.[9]

We see from the formula that increasing the weight of an aircraft is a significant factor. Doubling the weight will cut our rate of climb in half. A lighter aircraft will out-climb its heavier sister in direct proportion to the difference in weight.

The location of the centre of gravity also affects rate of climb. An aircraft with a more forward centre of gravity finds itself at a disadvantage compared to an identical aircraft at the same weight with a more aft centre of gravity. Moving the centre of gravity forward requires additional down-force developed by the tail-plane. This down-force acts on the aircraft like weight and effectively increases the total weight of the aircraft.

Density altitude significantly affects the climb performance of an aircraft. High density altitude, the performance altitude at which the machine is operating, reduces climb performance. Humidity, which can be factored into density altitude, also reduces performance, primarily through adversely affecting engine performance. High humidity results in reduced power output and thus reduced ETHP. A humid day with high density altitude may seriously decrease our ability to climb.

Use of carburetor heat reduces power output from the engine, which, in turn, reduces climb performance. Flaps increase lift but also increase drag. Use of flap on takeoff may shorten our ground run, but we pay for that advantage as soon as the wheels leave the surface. Increasing drag effectively reduces ETHP.

Landing gear, if you fly a machine capable of retracting its gear, also increases drag and thus reduces available excess thrust. To maximize climb performance with a retractable gear aircraft, let's get that gear up as soon as safely possible.

Angle of attack is critical to achieving climb performance. With a propeller driven aircraft the amount of available thrust decreases with airspeed due to the decreasing angle of attack on the propeller.[10] Increased airspeed rapidly increases parasite drag produced by the airframe, which, in turn, reduces ETHP.

To achieve maximum climb performance in terms of time, it is necessary to maintain an angle of attack resulting in best rate of climb speed, Vy. In terms of maximum altitude in relation to distance, we must maintain an angle of attack producing our best angle of climb speed, Vx. Turbulence and pilot skill both affect how well an aircraft maintains the correct angle of attack and thus airspeed to achieve best rate or best angle of climb.

Increasing or decreasing airspeed (angle of attack) above or below Vy or Vx decreases climb performance.

To minimize unpleasant surprises, if we do find ourselves flying in turbulent conditions, it would be an excellent plan to consider reduced performance in any calculation regarding obstacle clearance or time and distance to a given altitude.

It is important to note that Vy and Vx are not constant in terms of IAS as an aircraft gains altitude. A look at your machine's POH will give you some clues about this process. The 1976 C-172 POH, for example, recommends a best rate climb speed of 78 KIAS at sea level reducing to 75 KIAS at 3000', 72 KIAS at 6000', and only 68 KIAS at 10,000.

The speed and angle of attack for Vy is dependent on maximum excess thrust horsepower (excess power) and thus decreases with altitude. Vx, our best angle of climb speed, is dependent on maximum excess thrust (excess force). IAS for best angle of climb increases as we gain altitude.

Vy and Vx eventually converge as we approach our absolute ceiling, the altitude at which the machine's ability to climb at full power reaches zero.

A Rule of Thumb for estimating the decrease in Vy with altitude is to reduce indicated airspeed by 1% or 2 knots for each 1000' increase in altitude above sea level excluding the first 1000'. For Vx, a good Rule of Thumb is to increase indicated airspeed by ½% or 1/2 knot per 1000' or, more simply, 1 knot per 2000' increase in altitude.

To establish a cruise climb, the angle of climb we might use once we have achieved a safe altitude and are heading out on a cross country flight, we can simply add the difference between best angle of climb speed and best rate of climb speed to best rate of climb speed. For the C-172, for example, at 3000' the best rate of climb is 76 KIAS and best angle of climb is 60 KIAS; 76 − 60 + 76 = 92 or, more simply: two times Vy − Vx (2Vy − Vx). We can use this speed to maximize our distance made good and, at the same time, maintain a reasonable rate of climb.

Contrary to what many people suppose, climb is not produced by excess lift. Initially, pulling the nose up to enter a climb does briefly produce excess lift resulting in vertical acceleration. Once established in a steady state climb, however, it is excess thrust that causes an aircraft to climb, as our formula shows. In a steady state climb, our angle of attack will be identical to that for the same aircraft in level or descending flight at the same airspeed, assuming identical weight, centre of gravity location, and environmental conditions.

Intuitively, we might think that because we see a nose up attitude in a climb that our angle of attack must be greater than when flying straight and level. We don't want to confuse angle of climb with angle of attack or rate of climb, however.

Angle of climb is the angle of our flight path measured in relation to the horizon. Angle of attack is the angle described between the chord line of the wing and the relative wind. Our vertical speed, our rate of climb, is the aircraft's vertical velocity measured at right angles to the horizon.[11]

We can say that in a climb our attitude is a measure of our angle of climb plus our angle of attack. If, for example, in straight and level flight we maintain an angle of attack of, say, 7 degrees at a given airspeed, on entering a climb at an angle of 5 degrees at the same airspeed — about typical for a light training aircraft — our climb angle is now 5 degrees but our attitude in relation to the horizon is 7 + 5: 12 degrees.

So, do I as a pilot really need to know this stuff? Perhaps not. Understanding the machine's POH and allowing, always, a margin for safety normally does the job just fine.

Many people seem to fly happily and safely year in and year out without knowing very much at all. It is pretty cool stuff, however. I always figure you can always know too little, but it's impossible to know too much. The more we dig and learn about this miracle we call flight, the more interesting and compelling it all becomes.

Enjoy.

NOTES:

Chapter 1.7

The Climb Recovery

"Your attitude, not your aptitude, will determine your altitude."

-Zig Ziglan

One of the most basic and yet illusive skills we learn as pilots is to climb to a specified altitude, level off, and maintain the altitude. As flight instructors and pilot examiners, we see this skill in all its various forms on pre-solo check rides, private pilot, commercial pilot, multi-engine pilot, and instrument pilot flight tests. Indeed, I've watched it in my own performance. On my last instrument check ride, while climbing, turning, switching frequencies, and glancing, oh so briefly, down at the SID plate I blew right through my assigned altitude, gaining an unwanted extra 80 feet before pushing the nose down and recovering in a fairly undignified manner. Out of the side of my eye, I even managed to note a slight frown on the face of my examiner.

I suspect climb recovery is not one of those skills we, as instructors, teach extremely well. Somehow, many of us seem to think that a fifteen second lesson including the acronym APT: attitude, power, trim, does the job. Apparently, not quite as well as we might hope.

Whether you fly "on the gauges", as my friend Todd would say,[12] or while looking outside enjoying the miracle of flight as the good lord intended, learning to recover properly from a climb is actually a fairly complex manoeuvre, and understanding the process and the inherent dynamics pays off in the long term. For those pilots who have mastered this basic skill to a state of consistent excellence, good for you. For the rest of us mortals, a little review of this complex process can't hurt and might just do some good.

Right off the bat, an aeroplane climbs on excess thrust: climb is the result of the propulsion system producing more thrust than that required for level flight at a given airspeed. Every airspeed, we could say every angle of attack, requires a given amount of thrust for level flight. If we provide more thrust, the aeroplane climbs; if we reduce the thrust below that which is required, the aeroplane descends.[13]

Most typical training aircraft climb at a lower airspeed than they will normally be flown in cruise. The C-172, for example, might achieve Vy at sea level at around 75 KIAS, cruise climb at around 80-85 KIAS, and would cruise at around 100 KIAS. The C-172 simply does not have enough power to do much climbing at 100 KIAS. So, when levelling off, recovering from a climb, we are changing attitude, airspeed, and power all in a short period of time. Each of these changes produces some interesting dynamics, all of which must be controlled successfully for the climb recovery to look simple, feel smooth, and appear to be "under control".

So, let's explore.

A couple of very basic techniques can be very helpful in achieving success in a smooth, controlled climb recovery, and they won't hurt the rest of our flying a bit: holding the controls in the correct manner and trimming the aircraft properly. I have often wondered whether the bumpy parts on the backside of the control yoke or stick are the result of pilots using the classic death grip to hold the controls. I may well have been a contributor to that problem on several of the aeroplanes I have flown at one time or another. The problem with holding the control yoke or stick with an overly firm grip is that sensitivity is lost.

The tighter you hold the yoke or stick, the less clearly you are able to feel what the aeroplane is doing and the less sensitivity you have to maintain positive yet gentle control of the flight path. While the aeroplane may require a slightly firmer grip when manoeuvring than that used in cruise, refrain, as much as possible, from gripping the controls as though they were trying to escape with your last nickel. "Firm, positive, yet gentle" is the key phrase to keep in mind. Maintain your sensitivity to the flying machine's subtle messages.

Many experienced pilots recommend what might be termed a "pulsing grip" which involves holding the controls gently but firmly, then consciously relaxing your grip for a second or two to monitor the aircraft's behaviour. If it remains stable in the flight condition you are seeking, well and good. If it expresses an opinion about changing altitude, attitude, or heading, an adjustment to trim is called for. Keep repeating your pulsing grip throughout the flight and adjust trim, as required, whenever required.

Trimming the aeroplane for the attitude you want and need is one of the really critical skills in all aspects of flying. The untrimmed aeroplane develops an opinion which may well differ from yours. An improperly trimmed flying machine will fight you every inch of the way and make life much more difficult than necessary. Properly trimming a flying machine allows the controls to become essentially neutral and ready to accept small control inputs from the pilot, as required.

Proper trimming is not achieved as a one-time solution. It is an ongoing process. Any change, even minor, in the ambient environmental conditions — temperature, air density, vertical wind currents, humidity — all affect the aeroplane's interaction with its environment and will require appropriate adjustments in trim. The changing weight of the aircraft as it burns fuel, any shift in weights — a passenger shifting in his or her seat, for example, or any changes in power setting, will also require slight adjustments to trim setting. Your gentle touch on the control yoke or stick will transmit the aeroplane's need for readjusting trim if your fingers are light and easy on the yoke or stick.

Adjusting trim following any change in the correct order is also very helpful. Elevator trim is adjusted first to set the basic attitude for the flight condition you want to achieve. Next, adjust the rudder trim, if so equipped, and finally, adjust aileron trim, if so equipped. Remember to release your grip on the control yoke or stick following each adjustment to test how well you have achieved your goal of the perfectly trimmed aeroplane.

If your machine is not equipped with aileron and rudder trim — most light training aircraft are not — and it refuses to fly straight and level when left to its own devices after being properly trimmed, it may have developed some rigging issues which can, perhaps, become a discussion item between you and your favourite aircraft mechanic.

Sometimes, a slight tweak to the aileron activation rods, the adjustments for strut tension, or the fixed trim tab on the rudder can do wonders. Some years back, I spent something like three months tweaking the adjustment of the strut tension on a little Citabria I owned until I was finally happy to find she would fly hands off. It was worth the effort.

So, here we are in a nice, controlled, stable climb at, perhaps, 80 KIAS with a nose up angle of around 60, coming up to our specified altitude and getting ready to recover smoothly. Remember, changes in attitude, altitude, and power all require some lead time to execute properly. Our machine has momentum and would like to continue doing what it is doing; like most of us, it will resist change. It is our job, as the brains of the outfit, to manage that change with the least disruption possible.

The basic rule of thumb for recovery is the "lead" our inputs so change is smooth and controlled. We would like to level off, recover from the climb, at exactly the altitude we have been assigned or intend. For recovery from either a climb or a descent, 10% of our rate of climb, ROC or ROD, normally works very well. If we are climbing at 500'/minute, a pretty standard rate of climb for underpowered training aircraft, we will want to initiate our recovery from the climb about 50' before reaching our intended altitude. For IFR training, a standard call might be, "100 below" which gets us alerted to begin the process.

The recovery process requires that pitch angle, attitude, and power setting all change in a coordinated manner. Synchronizing all these changes is the tricky part, but it can be done, remembering throughout the procedure that changes to each of these three components will produce unwanted yaw tendencies which we will also want to anticipate and control.

Fifty feet below our intended altitude, we initiate the recovery process by lowering the nose half our angle of climb, in this case 30. The vertical speed of the aeroplane will quickly begin to decay, but the lag in our VSI indication will not really show this change right away. Our airspeed will begin to increase. As soon as the airspeed begins to increase, we will want to adjust our trim setting to help keep the nose down where we want it, and we can anticipate a slight yaw to the left caused by gyroscopic precession — changing the spatial orientation of the propeller much like the yaw experienced when lifting the tail of a conventional gear aircraft on takeoff — which we will compensate for with a touch of right rudder.[14]

At 25 feet below our intended altitude, we can lower the nose another 1.50, again half the nose up angle, adjust that trim again to keep the nose where we want it, anticipating the slight yaw tendency. Airspeed will be increasing; our rate of climb will be decreasing.

As we approach our intended altitude, our airspeed should be approaching cruise speed and our rate of climb should be approaching zero. As we reach altitude, we lower the nose to a zero climb angle and smoothly reduce power, as required, to our desired cruise power setting, remembering to anticipate and control any yaw tendencies that may arise; a reduction in power will have the tendency to produce a slight yaw to the right as slipstream is decreased, requiring a touch of left rudder to maintain heading. Here we are, so let's get this puppy trimmed correctly to maintain our new altitude and airspeed.

The short version: attitude, trim; attitude trim; attitude trim; attitude, power, trim. What could be simpler?

Whether you fly with reference inside or outside, learning to execute a smooth controlled climb recovery can make life so much easier and increase both your satisfaction in a job well done and bring smiles to those riding with you.

Enjoy.

NOTES:

Chapter 1.8

The Descent

"Here is Edward Bear, coming downstairs now, bump, bump, bump on the back of his head, behind Christopher Robin. It is, as far as he knows, the only way of coming downstairs, but sometimes he feels that there really is another way, If only he could stop bumping for a moment and think of it."

-A. A. Milne

Each and every flight in an aeroplane ends with a descent and re-acquaintance with the surface of our planet, one way or another. Since descending is an inevitable part of flight, it is in our interest as pilots to execute the manoeuvre in as skilful and purposeful manner as we can manage.

As Albert Einstein said, "Things should be made as simple as possible but not any simpler." While descending, a skill learned very early in the flight training process, seems simple and straightforward, there are a number of techniques that can be incorporated into our skill-set and a base of knowledge that can lead to improvement in our over-all performance as a pilot.

Executing a descent at the appropriate moment and in a skilful manner will improve both our enjoyment of flight and increase our safety.

We make use of the descent during several phases of flight. While enroute on a cross-country flight we must, at some point, execute a descent either to set up our approach for landing, to decrease altitude for weather, or to achieve a specified cruising altitude. We use the descent with power on approach and, either for practice or in the event of an engine failure, we descend with no engine power to assist us.

There are several generic factors affecting the way an aircraft descends. It is useful to understand them, so we can maintain precise control of the process. As with climb, the weight of the aircraft, the location of its centre of gravity, density altitude and humidity, use of carburetor heat, deployment of flaps and landing gear, turbulence, and the pilot's accuracy and skill in maintaining correct angle of attack and airspeed all affect an aircraft's descent.

An aircraft climbs proportionally to excess thrust; it descends proportionally to deficit thrust: the difference between thrust required to maintain level flight at a given airspeed and available thrust. In both climbs and descents, rate of altitude change is in inverse proportion to weight.

When talking about climb performance we use the formula Rate of Climb is equal to Excess Thrust Horsepower (ETHP) divided by weight, R/C = ETHP x 33,000/Weight, to determine our rate of climb at any given airspeed.[15] A descent can be thought of as a negative rate of climb so, using essentially the same formula, an aircraft's rate of descent (R/D), how quickly it loses altitude expressed in feet per minute (fpm), can be derived from the formula: R/D = Deficit Thrust Horse Power (DTHP) x 33,000/Weight.[16]

Weight is an interesting factor in relation to descent. At any given angle of climb—nose up attitude—a portion of the weight vector, which acts directly between the centre of gravity of the aeroplane and the centre of gravity of the planet, acts as drag and must be overcome by thrust. In a descent, a portion of the weight vector acts as thrust and assists us in our progress downward in direct proportion to our angle of descent. The steeper our angle of descent, the more weight provides assistance in increasing the rate of descent.

The lighter the machine is loaded, the less assistance is derived from weight at any given angle of descent, resulting in a lower rate of descent. Of course, at a 900 angle of descent—an exciting prospect—all the weight of the aircraft would be acting as though it were thrust. In a C-172 at gross weight with the engine turned off, we would have the equivalent of 2300 lbs. thrust acting straight down. We would discover the thrill of considerable vertical acceleration.

Centre of gravity location affects descent in the sense that an aircraft with a more forward centre of gravity is, effectively, a heavier aircraft resulting from the increase in down-force developed by the tail-plane, which acts on the aircraft as though it were weight. Centre of gravity is not something we normally have much control over during flight unless, perhaps, we have a load of skydivers, or, as my old buddy Duke Elegant used to say, a load of lobsters we can toss out the door, so we won't get too excited about it right now. We will simply remember that an aircraft with a more forward centre of gravity will descend at a slightly higher rate with a given power setting than the same aircraft with a more aft centre of gravity.

Density altitude and humidity affect rate of descent by increasing or decreasing drag. A high density altitude and high humidity environment — thinner air — results in reduced drag which, in turn, decreases the deficit thrust produced at any given power setting.

Once we are airborne, of course, there is not much we can do about the density altitude or humidity factors except understand how they affect performance.

Deployment of flap and landing gear increase drag. Increasing drag increases the amount of deficit thrust at any given power setting which increases our rate of descent.

If getting down at a higher rate of descent is a goal: get those flaps down and deploy the gear. We can also, of course, reduce power, increasing the amount of deficit thrust. Putting the machine into a slip also assists in increasing drag and thus increasing rate of descent. Use of carburetor heat decreases power output from the engine reducing available thrust and increasing our rate of descent.

Turbulence and pilot skill also affect rate of descent. This is particularly apparent in a glide, as angle of attack is very important. If we want to achieve minimum sink rate or maximum distance rate in a glide, maintaining the required airspeed and angle of attack is critical. Increasing or decreasing airspeed, angle of attack, will reduce our glide performance either in terms of time or distance.

When flying in turbulence, typically we choose to increase speed somewhat to ensure positive control of the machine, which, unfortunately, also changes performance. Increased airspeed increases our rate of descent in a glide or increases the amount of power required to maintain a given rate of descent. With the aircraft bouncing all about the sky, it may be a bit more challenging to maintain constant airspeed and angle of attack than when operating in still air.

But, what about my flight tomorrow?

When flying light aircraft, there are a few easy Rules of Thumb that can be a big help in setting up a desired descent profile. We know that attitude plus power gives us performance. The key factors we want to control in setting up the descent are the two control factors: power and attitude.

In level flight at cruise power, we remember that a change of 100 RPM or 1" MP results in a change in airspeed of approximately 5 knots. We know that the same change in RPM or MP, if we maintain the same airspeed, will result in a climb or descent at approximately 100'/min. So far, so good.

If I am flying at 100 knots and would like to establish a 300'/min rate of descent, I can reduce power by 300 RPM or 3" MP, adjust my attitude as required to maintain 100 knots, and the job is done. Some "fine tuning" may be required in the power setting, but the Rule of Thumb works pretty well for most light aircraft.

If I want to change airspeed and set up a rate of descent, for example from that 100 knots in cruise I would like to descend at 90 knots and 300'/min, I can reduce power 200 RPM or 2" MP for the airspeed change and an additional 300 RPM or 3" MP for the rate of descent: a total power reduction of 500 RPM or 5" MP. Once again, some "fine tuning" may be required.

Or, I can simply leave the power setting as is, poke the nose down, increasing airspeed to, say, 115 knots, and descend at 300'/min. I've already paid for my excess altitude. Why not get some of that cost back through an increase in airspeed?

One of the questions students always seem to struggle with is, "How do I know when to start my descent for approach?" For light aircraft there are a couple of easy Rules of Thumb that can see us through this dilemma.

For larger aircraft, typically people use some form of the 3/6 Rule: 3 times the altitude (in thousands of feet) you have to lose is the distance back to start the descent; 6 times your groundspeed is your descent rate. If I need to lose 5000' I would begin my descent 15 miles back (3 x 5 = 15); my descent rate at a ground speed of 100 knots would be 600'/min (100 x 6 = 600). This works well, but at higher speeds starts to give somewhat exciting rates of descent.

With light aircraft, 500'/min is a comfortable and fairly efficient rate of descent. Much faster and our ears start to pop and our passengers begin to get edgy. Much slower and it seems to take forever to reduce altitude.

A 500'/min rate of descent means two minutes to descend 1000'. If I am approaching my destination aerodrome at, say, 6500', and the circuit height is 1500', I will need to lose 5000'. I take the number of thousands, in this case 5, and multiply that number by 2 (5 x 2 = 10). This gives me the number of minutes back from the circuit I will need to begin my descent (10 minutes in this example).

To convert time to approximate distance we can simply multiply the time by our airspeed divided by 60. For example, if I am flying at 90 knots and have determined I need to initiate my descent 10 minutes prior to arrival at a selected point, I can multiply 10 by 90/60, or, more simply I can drop the extra zeros and multiply 10 by 9 and divide the result by 6, 15 miles. This is not exactly precise; my airspeed is not necessarily the same as my ground speed due to both wind factors and slant angle, but unless there is significant wind, the answer will do pretty nicely as a working solution.

So, here we are flying at 6500′ enroute Pitt Meadows – Campbell River. I check my CFS and determine airport elevation is 346′. Circuit altitude is 1300′ and I would like to be at circuit altitude at least 2 nm from the aerodrome. I need to lose 5200′ (6500 - 1300 = 5200). I determine I will need to initiate my descent procedure 11 minutes prior to arrival (5.2 times 2 = 10.4). I round up just to keep things simple. If I am descending at 100 knots I will need to initiate descent approximately 20 nm from the aerodrome (11 x 100/60 = 18.3 + 2 = 20).[17]

As I cross the line between Cape Lazlo and Harwood Island, I can reduce power approximately 500 RPM or 5″ MP, set up my descent profile at 500′/min, get everything all trimmed in and allow the machine to descend to my intended altitude of 1300′ in good time to enter the pattern at Campbell River. No muss, no fuss.

If your brain doesn't appreciate math during flight—pretty normal for most people—make a plan prior to flight. No need to make this difficult. Planning ahead is always a good idea in any case. It saves all sorts of confusion later. If you already know what you will need to do, all you have to do in the aircraft is execute the plan.

On approach to landing, a standard approach profile, the 30 glide slope can be achieved by setting up a rate of descent at 5 times your ground speed. If I am approaching at, say, 60 knots, a rate of descent of 300 fpm should set me up nicely.

Keep things simple. Plan and think ahead.

Enjoy.

NOTES:

(Endnotes)

1 Kershner, William K., The Advanced Pilot's Flight Manual, Sixth Edition, Iowa State University Press, Ames, Iowa, USA, 1994, pg.7.

2 1 Horse Power = 550 ft-lbs/second or 33,000 ft-lbs/minute

3 1 Horse Power = 550 ft-lbs/second or 33,000 ft-lbs/minute

4 Imeson, Sparky, Mountain Flying, Airguide Publications, Inc., Long Beach, California, 1994, pg. 13

5 http://selair.selkirk.ca/Training/Program_Manual/documents/ Private Pilot Course.pdf page 47

6 Technically, Va is the maximum speed at which application of full aerodynamic control inputs will not overstress the aeroplane. Larger aircraft use Maximum Gust Intensity Speed, Vb(min), the speed at which the aircraft can sustain a vertical gust of 66'/sec without stalling and Vb(max) the speed at which the aeroplane can sustain a gust of 66'/ min without overstressing the aircraft and Vra, Rough Air Speed, the recommended speed for flight in turbulent air. Light aircraft normally use Va as the maximum speed for both full deflection of controls and turbulent air penetration speed.

7 http://www.tc.gc.ca/eng/civilaviation/regserv/cars/part5-standards-chapter523a-1927.htm

8 Spronk, John, "Flying in Turbulent Air", unpublished article, 1996

9 Kershner, William K., The Advanced Pilot's Flight Manual, Iowa State University Press, 1994, page 90. We can work this formula backward and determine that a C-172 which climbs at 645 fpm at gross weight at sea level can develop approximately 45 excess thrust horsepower at best rate of climb speed. One horsepower equals 550 ft lb/ sec or 33,000 foot pounds per minute.

10 Esser, Dave, "Aircraft Climb Performance," Woman Pilot Magazine, August 2002.

11 Todd Pezer, http://www.betterpilots.com/3.html12

13 For those interested in these things, the relationship between thrust and climb is: Sin (climb angle) = (Thrust – Drag)/Weight.

14 Cool video on Gyroscopic Precession: http://youtu.be/ ty9QSiVC2g0

15 Kershner, William K., The Advanced Pilot's Flight Manual, Iowa State University Press, 1994, page 90. One horsepower equals 550 ft lb/ sec or 33,000 foot pounds/min.

16 Kershner, William K., The Advanced Pilot's Flight Manual, Iowa State University Press, 1994, page 34. One horsepower equals 550 ft lb/sec or 33,000 foot pounds/min. If you find these things interesting, a Rate of Descent of 500'/min at constant airspeed will require a reduction in power of approximately 35 hp (500 = 33000 x DTHP/33000; DTHP = 34.85 hp).

17 Using the 3/6 Rule: 5.2 x 3 = 15.6, call it 16nm, + 2 = 17 nm back from destination. 6 x 100 knots = 600'/min for rate of descent.

PART 2: FLIGHT MANOEUVRES

Chapter 2.1

Exploring the Stall: The Basic, Level Stall

"One of the greatest discoveries a man makes, one of his greatest surprises, is to find he can do what he was afraid he couldn't."
-Henry Ford

The aerodynamic stall is a very interesting phenomenon and an important one with which to be familiar. Most pilots are not particularly keen to stall their aircraft just for the fun of it, and a surprising number—I discover this doing checkouts—have not taken the time to stall an aircraft intentionally since their last flight test.

Of course, we never want to stall an aircraft unintentionally at any time, but having a good understanding of the stall characteristics and the symptoms leading up to the stall for the aircraft you are flying can be information that might save your life.

An aircraft wing stalls at a particular angle of attack. That's the whole story. The stall is not a function of airspeed, although we commonly practice stall entry at low airspeed, nor is it a function of attitude, although we generally associate the stall with a nose up attitude as a result of our training sessions. A stall happens because the angle of attack of the wing—the angle between the chord line of the wing and the relative wind—has exceeded the critical angle.

In training, I sometimes use the metaphor of ice formation: water freezes under normal conditions at 0^0C. At 1^0C, water is not frozen. It is the same with the stall. Below the critical angle of attack, the wing is not stalled. Above the critical angle, the wing stalls.

How do we recover from a stall? We reduce the angle of attack. If we're right side up, we move the stick forward, lowering the nose. If we're upside down, we pull the stick back, lowering the nose. If we're in a normal, outside turn, we ease the stick forward, lowering the nose. In any situation, what we do to recover from the onset of a stall is reduce the angle of attack below the critical angle that is producing the stall.

For those few aviators who still mess about with conventional gear aircraft, understanding and having an accurate feeling for the onset of the stall is very important. Every time we settle into a nice three-point landing we are, essentially, stalling the aircraft onto the runway.

Most conventional gear, tailwheel, aircraft are designed so that the angle of attack achieved when the aircraft is sitting on all three wheels is the critical angle of attack that results in a stalled condition, or just slightly more. For the odd one with short legs, like the little Citabria flown by a friend of mine, the three-point landing can become an interesting challenge because, in the three-point attitude, his aircraft is not at or beyond the critical angle of attack.

For tricycle gear aircraft, the stall angle is somewhat less critical for landing. The aircraft is generally not stalled onto the runway except, perhaps, by beginning students who may flair a bit high. Normally, with tricycle gear aircraft, we fly them onto the landing surface just above the stall to ensure positive control of the machine. We establish and maintain an attitude the provides minimum sink rate just prior to touchdown.

With any aircraft, however, it is very important to know and be familiar with the symptoms of an approaching stall, so we can make positive decisions on how to proceed. If it is your intention to stall the aircraft: excellent. Proceed with the manoeuvre. If it is not your intention to stall the aircraft, notice the approaching stall and correct the problem by reducing the angle of attack before the stall occurs.

It's like knowing, in the dark, where the edge of the stairs is at home. If you know exactly where the edge is, you can approach it with confidence; if you are unsure, you may well step over by mistake and find yourself in deep, deep trouble.

When we practice stalls in training, we do them at altitude where there will be no problems. Even if we do a poor job of recovering from the manoeuvre, we have plenty of altitude to play with and no harm results. If, however, we inadvertently stall the aircraft low to the ground, on landing or approach for example, we can find ourselves in a world of hurt. Add a touch of yaw to that picture and we are in real trouble.

If you are flying an aircraft that is new to you, or if it's been a while since you practiced basic stalls, it might be an excellent idea to investigate them again. If you have any qualms about the manoeuvre, find an instructor you trust and feel comfortable flying with, and ask him or her to take you up to practice a few stalls.

Basic power-off stalls with no power and power-on recoveries are a great place to start.

Complete your safety checks, HASEL, HALT, CALL or whatever system you were taught, making certain all is safe and correct. Do a good lookout. Remember that this manoeuvre will lose some altitude so have a good look below. Apply the carburetor heat, ease the power back to idle, and hold your altitude by increasing the angle of attack as you slow down.

There is no need to aggressively pull back on the stick. Doing so actually makes it more difficult to see, feel, and hear the approach to the stall, which is what we really want to understand and know.

Pick a reference point, if at all possible, so you can monitor closely any yaw that may develop. A cloud or a mountain peak will work just fine. If it is a clear, beautiful blue sky, you may have to monitor the directional gyro or magnetic compass, but these are not as sensitive as your eye on a fixed point outside. We want to avoid any unintentional yaw if we can.

As the aircraft approaches its critical angle of attack, take note of the developing symptoms. You will see a slight nose up attitude. If your aircraft is equipped with one, you will hear the stall warning begin about 10 Knots or so ahead of the actual stall. You will begin to feel a slight buffeting on the stick caused by the disturbed air coming off the wings and hitting the horizontal stabilizer. The controls will feel quite sluggish and unresponsive. You will note the quiet resulting from reduced airflow over the aircraft and the idling engine.

At the stall itself, the nose may drop slightly. If you are very gentle in your approach to the stall, you may not notice any significant nose drop, but you will have full aft deflection of the yoke or stick and the aircraft will begin losing altitude. If you have not been attentive to the rudder controls and have allowed yaw to develop, the aircraft may show you it has been yawing by dropping a wing.

So, we've achieved a nice power-off stall. Let's recover.

If we wish to recover from the stall without power, we simply reduce the angle of attack.

Once again, no need to be overly aggressive. We don't need to bounce our poor instructor's head off the headliner. We simply need to reduce the angle of attack below the critical angle so the aircraft is flying again. Normally, a slight nose down attitude will do the job nicely. We're now in a gentle glide.

If we wish to recover with power, we reduce the angle of attack and give the aircraft full power, being alert to control the adverse yaw produced by torque and slipstream. Don't forget to close the carburetor heat after applying power.

Normally, lowering the nose to approximately cruise attitude or slightly below will be sufficient if we are using power. As soon as we can confirm positive airspeed, we can regain our lost altitude and carry on.

Practicing stalls so you can learn, understand, and know the stall characteristics of your aircraft will give you a sense of control and security. You will know where the edge is and will be able to approach it with confidence. You will know the symptoms of the approaching stall and know how and when to modify your inputs to either produce or avoid the stall, as required.

Your landings will improve, your flying will improve, and your sense of your own knowledge and skills will boost your confidence.

The basic stall is a simple yet elegant and important procedure. If you're not completely comfortable with stalls, now is an excellent time to find whatever assistance you may need to develop a positive relationship with the manoeuvre.

You'll be glad you did.

NOTES:

Chapter 2.2

Exploring the Stall: Some Advanced Stalls

"Experience is a hard teacher because she gives the test first, the lesson afterward."

-Vernon Law, baseball pitcher

In Chapter 2.1 we explored some aspects of the basic, level power off stall.

Of course, we never want to stall an aircraft unintentionally at any time, but having a good understanding of the stall characteristics and the symptoms leading up to the stall for the aircraft you are flying can be information that might save your life.

As we discussed, an aircraft wing stalls at a particular angle of attack. That's the whole story. The stall is not a function of airspeed, although we commonly practice stall entry at low airspeed, nor is it a function of attitude, although we generally associate the stall with a nose up attitude as a result of our training sessions. A stall happens because the angle of attack of the wing — the angle between the chord line of the wing and the relative wind — has exceeded the critical angle.

We also discussed stall recovery. How is it accomplished? Reduce the angle of attack. If we're right side up, we move the stick forward, lowering the nose. If we're upside down, we pull the stick back, lowering the nose. If we're in a normal, outside turn, we ease the stick forward to reduce the angle of attack in relation to the relative wind, and, if we can, we reduce the angle of bank to reduce the load factor, which reduces stall speed.

In any situation, to recover from the onset of a stall, reduce the angle of attack below the critical angle that is producing the stall.

We discussed the symptoms of the approaching stall and the importance of knowing and recognizing them before the actual stall arrives, so we can make a decision about whether or not we choose to allow the aircraft to stall. What are we looking, listening, and feeling for? Loss of positive control responses, the buffet caused by roiled air striking the horizontal stabilizer, perhaps the stall warning horn or light if the aircraft is so equipped.

At the stall itself, of course, the nose will drop as we lose lift and control response, but unless we are performing a stall on purpose, we'd like to recognize its approach and solve the problem before it occurs.

It's like knowing, in the dark, where the edge of a curb is. If you know exactly where the edge is you can approach it with confidence; if you are unsure, you may well step over by mistake and find yourself in trouble.

More advanced stalls, rather than the basic level stall are, generally, the ones that get pilots into trouble. They arrive while we are doing something else, like trying to avoid trees, or check out the babes on the beach, or losing an engine on takeoff, or, perhaps, trying to turn in a confined area.

We won't even discuss getting into trouble as a result of attempting to prove that you're just as good as Patty Wagstaff. Just be smart. Fly within your limits, or get some help from a competent person to help you explore more advanced manoeuvres.

Let's take a look at three of the advanced stalls typically associated with difficulties: the departure stall, the arrival stall, and the accelerated stall.

The departure stall results from pulling too hard into a climb. Some of the frequent causes of this type of stall are avoiding obstacles on takeoff or, in low level flight, avoiding birds or other aircraft; showing off; wind shear; wing contamination; or becoming distracted and allowing airspeed to decay unnoticed followed by an abrupt change in attitude.

The guidance notes for flight instructors[1] give a description of a typical departure stall accident: "Location: 1,100' grass strip with 75' high pine trees at departure end of the runway. The departing C-150 was observed by witnesses to become airborne approximately 200' from the end of the strip and approximately 500' from a line of pine trees off the departure end of the strip. The aircraft entered a steep climbing right turn then rolled to the left and descended in a steep nose down attitude until it collided with the ground. Two fatal."

The pilot, seeing that he or she would not be able to clear the trees, attempted to increase the climb rate by pulling back on the control column. The aircraft reached and exceeded its critical angle of attack and stalled. At the same time, as the pilot pulled back he or she entered a turn to the right. The aircraft stalled, dropped its high wing, because that wing will have had a slightly higher angle of attack than the lower wing in a turn so will stall first, and spun to the left. From 200' the pilot did not have had the necessary altitude to recover from the spin.

At 3000', a departure stall can be a surprising event if you are not prepared. At 200', it is too often fatal. If you haven't practiced one since your flight test, it's not a bad plan to find a safe altitude in a safe location and try a few for practice. If you're not certain of the whole idea, take your friendly local flight instructor up with you. The important thing is to know and recognize the symptoms of the stall's approach. A little work with your aircraft's POH regarding obstacle clearance takeoffs isn't a totally bad plan, either.

The arrival stall, sometimes described as a descending, turning stall, results when a pilot, normally at low altitude, possibly on final approach or turning base to final, allows the airspeed to decay and some yaw to develop. Some typical scenarios for the arrival stall are turning to correct for an overshoot of the extended runway centerline; turning to avoid obstacles, birds, or other aircraft; attempting to stretch a glide to the runway by raising the nose and not applying power; illusions in strong wind conditions; and distraction resulting in airspeed decay.

From the guidance notes we have an example: "Location: 1 mile east of Fairfax aerodrome. Weather conditions: VFR, winds NW at 15 Knots, moderate turbulence. The Piper Cub J-3 overshot the extended centerline for runway 26 while turning final. Witnesses observed the aircraft turning from south to the west at a moderate bank angle. Prior to completion of the turn the aircraft's bank attitude increased rapidly and the nose dropped to a nearly vertical attitude. The wreckage impact was consistent with an aircraft in a spin condition. One fatal."

At 3000', or whatever might be required for safe altitude, some practice will show you the edges of your own aircraft's descending turn stall. You will see and come to recognize the approaching symptoms so you will never do one at low level when the results will not be just a bit of a surprise. Unlike the departure stall, in a descending turning stall the inside or down wing will stall first. It is traveling slightly slower through the air and reaches its critical angle of attack before the up wing, leading to a spin in the direction of the turn. It is slightly less dramatic than the departure stall but can be no less fatal if it occurs at the wrong time in the wrong place.

An accelerated stall is frequently entered from a level turn and results, as with all stalls, from too high an angle of attack. The added factor we must consider with an accelerated stall is the increased wing loading or load factor resulting from acceleration. In a turn, we are accelerating; the loading on the wings is increased by a function of the angle of bank.

Without beating the math to death, we might remember from ground school that a 45° bank turn produces a 1.41g loading; a 60° bank turn produces a 2g loading and a 75° bank turn results in a 4g loading. We can look these values up and save ourselves some effort, or we can work them out ourselves. We can derive them either mathematically or geometrically. Mathematically, we find that $G = 1/\cos \theta$ (where θ = the angle of bank). One divided by the cosine of our angle of bank is the multiplier of our weight to find live load or "G" force.

The stall speed, we may also remember, increases by the square root of the "G" force, or load factor on the aircraft so that, in a 60° bank turn, our stall speed increases by the square root of 2, 1.41. If your normal un-accelerated stall speed in level flight is 50 Knots, your stall speed in a 60° bank turn will be 70.7 Knots.

When might an accelerated stall occur? Typically, the pilot sightseeing at low level, the pilot turning to look at landmarks, wildlife, people (remember those babes on the beach?), or turning to avoid obstacles or other aircraft may produce the necessary conditions.

A classic example is provided in the instructor guidelines: "Location: 2 miles west of Clarence Lake. Weather conditions: VFR. The Cessna 210 with 3 persons onboard was observed to be flying at tree top level and manoeuvring in an abrupt manner. A video camera recovered from the wreckage recorded the final minutes of the flight. The pilot was manoeuvring to allow a passenger to video tape a moose when the stall warning horn activated and the aircraft stalled in a 45° left bank turn at an altitude of 50 feet AGL. Three fatal."

Practicing stalls so you can learn, understand, and know the stall characteristics of your aircraft will give you a sense of control and security. You will know where the edges are and will be able to approach them with confidence. You will know the symptoms of the approaching stall and know how and when to modify your inputs to either produce or avoid the stall, as required.

Don't allow that surprise unplanned stall to be the first one of its type you experience. Under safe, controlled conditions at a comfortable and safe altitude is an excellent place to practice some advanced stalls so the symptoms and indications are clear and fresh in your mind and body and the recovery procedures are also second nature. It might just save your life and the lives of those who put their trust in you to pilot them safely.

OK. It's also a bit of fun.

NOTES:

Chapter 2.3

Gliding

"Touch us gently, Time! Let us glide adown thy stream. Gently, - as we sometimes glide through a quiet dream!"

-Barry Cornwall

Gliding is a manoeuvre rarely practiced by most of us once flight training is completed. Even during pilot training, gliding is often dealt with in a somewhat perfunctory manner. The forced approach exercise is, by far, the most commonly failed item on flight tests, according to Transport Canada statistics. I certainly notice when checking out even very experienced pilots that gliding often proves a challenging endeavour.

Understanding the basic mechanics of the glide and incorporating gliding practice into our routine as a pilot can improve both skills and safety. Competence requires two factors: correct training and practice. Hopefully, each of us will have had adequate training at some point in our pilot careers. Practice to maintain and improve skills once training is completed is up to each one of us. The thought of having an engine failure 10 years after the last time we made an opportunity to practice gliding doesn't instil confidence.

In the not too distant past, power-off landing approaches with light aircraft were standard practice and provided gliding practice on each landing. The reliability of aircraft engines has improved greatly, and with both light and heavier aircraft, the power-on stabilized approach has become standard. This practice has made landings a more certain endeavour, but it has reduced the opportunity for pilots to practice gliding on a regular basis.

For the most part, we have to consciously seek out opportunities to practice this very important skill to keep ourselves current and competent.

The three major factors we can consider as affecting glide are aircraft weight, angle of attack, and wind. Aircraft weight is an interesting factor in relation to gliding. We discussed this aspect in a previous article when we talked about descents.

In normal flight, there are four forces acting on an aeroplane: lift, weight, thrust, and drag. In a glide, we encounter the unique situation of dealing with only three forces: lift, weight, and drag. Thrust is absent. In a true glide, our engine is stopped; no thrust is being produced.

If we draw the little triangles to help understand the forces active in a glide, we notice the aircraft assumes a nose down, descending path. Lift acts upwards at right angles to the direction of flight; drag acts opposite and parallel to the direction of flight; weight acts directly between the centre of gravity of the machine and the centre of gravity of the earth.

A portion of the weight vector, what we call its horizontal component, acts not as thrust but as though it was thrust, parallel and in the same direction as our line of travel. The steeper our angle of descent, the more weight provides assistance as though it were thrust, overcoming drag and increasing airspeed. The greater the weight of the aeroplane, the more assistance we derive. In a vertical dive—hold on to your hats—all our weight would act as though it were thrust.

Our glide ratio, the ratio between distance over the ground and altitude lost, is equal to our lift-to-drag ratio.[2] In order to maximize the distance we travel over the ground in a glide, we must achieve the best possible lift-to-drag ratio.[3] We may remember something similar from our study of flight for maximum range when we also looking to achieve the best lift-to-drag ratio.[4]

The angle of attack for best lift-to-drag ratio is fixed. Since lift must equal weight in a steady state non-accelerated manoeuvre, the only variable left to manipulate, for us as pilots, is airspeed.[5]

Very few light training aeroplanes are fitted with an angle of attack meter, so we use airspeed as our primary source of information regarding angle of attack. When gliding, we achieve best lift-to-drag angle of attack at different airspeeds depending on the weight of the machine. A heavier machine will achieve best lift-to-drag at the same angle of attack as a lighter one but will do so at a higher airspeed.

Regardless of weight, two identical machines starting at the same altitude in the same environmental conditions will arrive on the ground at the same spot, having traveled exactly the same distance over the ground. The heavier machine, however, will arrive more quickly. It's sort of counterintuitive, but there it is, and we have the math to prove it.

Wind is a very important factor when gliding and should be considered carefully when making a plan to arrive at a given point on the surface. We all know wind affects ground speed, how fast we travel over the surface, but does not affect airspeed. As William Kershner points out, in the event of an emergency, we will probably be better off not overcomplicating an already complicated situation. [6]

However, increasing airspeed slightly when gliding into a headwind or reducing it slightly when gliding with a tailwind will increase distance traveled over the ground.

An easy Rule of Thumb to keep in mind is to increase glide speed into a headwind by one-half the headwind speed. In most cases, particularly if there is any turbulence, it is not practical to slow the aircraft down very much in a tailwind as we are already flying at low speed, and stall protection is always a healthy concept.

With a headwind, time is the enemy. We want to minimize the amount of time the headwind is working against us. With a tailwind, time is our friend.

In an emergency, a better plan would most likely be to pick a landing site that does not require us to get every possible inch out of our glide, if that is an option.

There are two basic types of glide most often considered: the minimum sink rate glide and the maximum distance glide. Gliding for minimum sink rate is used to achieve maximum time in the air at the sacrifice of distance. This can be a useful manoeuvre in particular situations. You might find yourself without power over flat ground, water, snow, or a marshy area where altitude is difficult to judge and arriving at a particular point is not be a priority.

The speed for minimum sink rate glide is closely related to the speed for maximum endurance. The match is not exact because, even at the minimal power setting for maximum endurance, the propeller is providing thrust and increasing the airflow over the inside portion of the wings and the aircraft's tail section. With the power off, the thrust and slipstream produced by even minimal power is absent, and the propeller itself, if it is allowed to windmill, creates significant drag.

The minimum sink rate glide has both the advantages and disadvantages of low airspeed. On the plus side, we will have as much time as possible to assess our situation, take positive action, and we will arrive at the surface at as low an air speed as possible. This can be of great benefit to our survival: impact increases with the square of the speed at contact (F=ma).

When gliding to land, perhaps at night or in low visibility on a surface that may be difficult to assess, low speed is all to the good. Float pilots may be able to relate this process to glassy water landings when it is challenging to assess altitude above the surface prior to contact. The key is to establish a low and stabilized rate of descent at low airspeed consistent with maintaining control of the aeroplane and a low rate of descent.

On the down side, control problems may easily arise in turbulent conditions, necessitating a higher airspeed, which reduces time in the air.

A basic Rule of Thumb for the minimum sink rate glide for single engine, fixed gear aeroplanes is to use 1.1 x Vs (KCAS) factored for weight (√aircraft weight/gross weight). Not something we would want to calculate moments after the engine quits on a dark night over the ocean, but something we could spend a moment with on a rainy day in the comfort of our living room or office and perhaps record on our checklist for future reference in the event of need.

The maximum distance glide is probably a more commonly used number. It is closely associated with the speed for maximum range, but, as with the minimum sink rate glide, is not exactly the same. Your machine's POH will normally provide a generic number you can learn and use in the event you want to practice or must execute a glide prior to a forced landing.

The basic Rule of Thumb for the maximum distance glide for single engine, fixed gear aeroplanes is to use 1.3 x Vs (KCAS) factored for weight. Once again, I can't see myself pulling out a calculator in the event of an engine failure, but playing with the numbers in a safe place where time is not a factor does seem to help increase appreciation for where those numbers come from.

The reality is that a couple of knots one way or the other will have no significant affect: there is no point, operationally, in getting too finicky about the whole problem.

As an example, a quick look in the POH for a 1976 C-172M tells me "best glide speed" is 65 KIAS (66 KCAS) with flaps up and 60 KIAS with flaps down. Going back to the Rule of Thumb, assuming gross weight, I calculate glide for maximum distance with a most forward C of G as 65 KCAS. With a most aft C of G, it calculates as 68.9 KCAS.

Averaging the two numbers comes out to 66.95 KCAS; call it 67 KCAS. Pretty close to Cessna's numbers.

Just for the fun of it, I can factor for weight and find, at 2100 lbs., maximum distance glide will be executed at 64 KCAS (rounded off); at

1900 lbs., it is 61 KCAS (rounded off). Not terribly significant differences, but there they are.

On a practical note, practicing the glide will keep required skills and techniques current and provide an opportunity to improve those skills. It also allows us to develop a greater sense of confidence in performing the manoeuvre should it become necessary or useful. Playing with the machine for practice when we are not faced with the stress of an emergency allows us to get a much more solid handle on the whole problem and develop a much clearer sense of what can or must be done to maximize the performance of a particular machine.

A policeman doesn't want to start learning how to use his pistol moments after being confronted by an armed felon; a school doesn't want to start practicing fire drills immediately following the discovery of smoke billowing from the furnace room.

It's an excellent idea to prevent your next gliding practice session from occurring years after the last time you tried it just following an unexpected stoppage of that little fan up front. How much fun does a person really need, after all?

Enjoy.

NOTES:

Chapter 2.4

Slipping

"On the other hand there is always a good chance of slide-slipping your airplane down in such a way that you fan the flames away from yourself and the wings."

-Major Raoul Lufbery
Lafayette Escadrille, May 1918

As Major Raoul Lufbery, a celebrated WWI American ace credited with 17 aerial victories over German aircraft on the Western Front, pointed out only a few days prior to his death, the slip can be a very useful manoeuvre. Unfortunately for the Major, when the fuel tank of his Nieuport 28 was hit by tracer fire from a German Albatross on May 19, 1918, he ignored his own advice and jumped from the burning aircraft at 200', apparently hoping to land in a nearby stream. He was impaled on a picket fence.

If you spend any time flying with older pilots, those who learned to fly in the bad old days when an aircraft's third wheel was normally bolted to the rear end rather than hanging down at the front end, you will likely have watched someone who was very familiar and comfortable executing slipping manoeuvres. Back in the day, when flaps were an expensive complexity not seen on small training aircraft, slipping was both taught and learned thoroughly from the very first flights.

Pilots were taught to use a slip to lose altitude, either straight ahead or in a turn, and on landing to compensate for crosswind drift. As a friend of mine said, when you're flying a tail wheel aircraft with a gross weight of 1220 lbs., every landing is a crosswind landing. If someone drops a sheet of plywood on a construction site across the road from the aerodrome, you feel it. A slip is also a handy manoeuvre to just get a better view of something on the ground or above the wing or even to help you re-latch a door opened in flight.

With some of the older machines, the Stearman for example, where the pilot sits in the aft seat with most of the aeroplane and a big radial engine obscuring forward vision, the typical approach technique is to reduce power to idle abeam the threshold and enter a slipping turn into base and final so a view of the runway or landing area is available. Once the aeroplane is established in a landing attitude and lined up with the runway, forward vision is blocked; the runway disappears from view.

Modern training aircraft are almost universally equipped with flaps, and most instructors learned to fly from instructors who learned to fly on tricycle gear aircraft, also equipped with flaps. Flaps are a great help when altitude must be lost and actually improve forward vision. With flaps deployed the machine will fly in a more nose down attitude; tricycle gear aircraft are not nearly as vulnerable to difficulties as conventional gear aircraft when landed somewhat askew in crosswind conditions. Slipping has gently faded as a favoured technique.

It is, however, still a very useful manoeuvre and quite elegant, when performed correctly.

Whether we are speaking about a side slip used to counteract crosswind drift on landing, a forward slip used to lose altitude, or a slipping turn used to lose lots of altitude and change direction at the same time the essentials of the technique is the same. With a combination of aileron and rudder inputs, we induce the aircraft to fly sideways through the air. We transfer some of the lift from the wings to the fuselage and create a significant amount of drag in the process.

When we use a slipping technique to counter crosswind drift on landing, a side slip, we point the nose of the aircraft with rudder input to keep the longitudinal axis of the machine parallel to the centreline of the runway or landing area and apply aileron to maintain lateral position. Rudder points the nose; ailerons slide the aircraft right or left, as needed. Of course, we use elevator and trim to control our approach speed and power to control our rate of descent. The increase in drag resulting from the slip typically requires more power than a normal approach if we are to maintain a normal rate of descent.

When using the slip to lose altitude, a forward slip, we normally enter from a power-off glide. All too often on a flight test, we see people enter a slip to lose altitude with cruise or only slightly reduced power. This defeats the technique. With enough power, we can fly the aircraft with full rudder and opposite aileron without losing any altitude at all.

To maximize altitude loss, we need to fly the aeroplane at a reduced speed to give the slipping manoeuvre time to be effective. Slipping increases the rate of descent, but if we increase our speed over the ground much of the benefit of the slip is lost.

The German Fieseler Storch, a light observation aircraft of WWII vintage, was capable of slipping its way to landing in a stalled condition, enabling the pilot to execute a safe landing in very minimal distance. Please don't try this trick with your C-172, however.

To execute a slip to lose altitude, we establish the aircraft in a glide, normally at best glide speed as specified in the POH. Once in the glide, it is very important to establish and maintain a clear visual reference so we know where we are headed. I like to pick out an obvious and prominent feature on the ground ahead—about where we would touch down if we continued our descent—and maybe even say out loud or to myself, "That's where I'm going."

We also want to take note of the aircraft's attitude. Once in a slip, depending on the aircraft we are flying, the airspeed indicator may become unreliable. The airspeed indicator is designed to display ram air pressure calibrated in knots or miles per hour, the total pressure provided by the pitot tube minus the static pressure provided by the static port. In a slip, the pitot tube and static port are now meeting the relative airflow at unusual angles.

In a C-172, for example, the static port is located on the forward left side of the fuselage. In a slip to the left, airflow into the static port is increased and airflow into the pitot tube is decreased, resulting in the indicated airspeed reading low. In a right slip, the opposite becomes true: the indicated airspeed reading is increased.

If we practice looking outside to establish and maintain attitude, we won't be confused or fooled by inaccurate indicated airspeed readings.

With our eyes on our reference point and an appreciation of the attitude of the nose, we can apply aileron in the direction we would like to establish our slip. Left aileron results in a slip to the left; right aileron results in a slip to the right. We roll the aircraft with aileron and stop the turn with opposite rudder: roll left: right rudder. Roll right: left rudder.

Particularly in the early stages of learning this manoeuvre, gentle application of control inputs is easier to understand and manage. Remember to maintain visual reference with our destination. No big hurry. Strive for elegance and smooth control inputs rather than speed.

As we enter the slip, the aircraft may have a tendency to raise its nose. We are increasing lift by exposing the whole side of the aircraft to the relative wind. Maintain the attitude we observed in the glide with elevator input. Keep eyes on our ground reference point so we continue to know where we're heading.

Many students are worried about stalling the aircraft and producing a spin because of the cross control inputs and have a tendency to point to nose excessively downward. This simply increases speed and reduces the effectiveness of the slip.

Most light aircraft are very reluctant to spin from a slip. If you are really worried about it, give yourself plenty of altitude in a safe area and try it. Put the aircraft into a slip and gently raise the nose until she stalls. Most light aircraft will shake and buffet and lose altitude at a great rate, but they will not show any interest whatsoever in spinning. Recovery is easy: lower the nose just enough so the buffeting stops and you are re-established on your glide path toward your ground reference point.

In the early stages of learning to slip, I encourage students to use full rudder input and "steer" the aircraft with aileron. This simplifies things by giving the pilot only one input to worry about and control. Two variable variables result in so many combinations that it's easy to get confused. Keep things simple, and success is more easily obtained.

If there is a wind blowing, we normally set ourselves up with the lowered wing towards the wind. This is particularly important when using a slipping manoeuvre on approach in gusty conditions. With limited altitude, we don't want to increase our vulnerability by giving the wind an opportunity to get under the raised wing and toss us into an unusual and potentially dangerous attitude.

To turn our slip into a slipping turn, simply increase aileron input. A slipping turn can be a very effective tool for losing altitude in a hurry and can be a very nice little trick to store in our forced landing kit or our landing kit for fields with difficult or obstructed approach paths. We can really keep our base in close by making use of the slipping turn in an effective manner.

Whether you are an experienced pilot or a new arrival to the activity, honing and developing skills is not only an excellent plan, it's a lot of fun. Slips can be extremely useful in a variety of situations. Familiarity and comfort with the manoeuvre is a fine addition to your repertoire. Flaps fail; crosswinds occur; engines catch fire; difficult situations arise. Keep your skills sharp and they will be there for you when you need them.

NOTES:

Chapter 2.5

Understanding the Spin

"...in practice stalls and spins the ground only says, "boo"; in the real thing it comes after you.

-Leighton Collins

I remember all too well my first experience with a spin. We had been practicing slow flight and stalls when my instructor asked me to climb to 4000' AGL. He took control of the aircraft and said, with a big smile, "I'm going to show you something."

He abruptly pulled the nose up and jammed in full left rudder. The aircraft rolled upside down; both doors popped open; the nose pointed straight down at the fields below. The world began to spin violently around; details in the fields below grew clearer in a big hurry.

He recovered from the manoeuvre and helped me close the doors. Turning to me he asked, "Are you OK?" "Not really," I replied as I began to re-consider my decision to earn a pilot licence.

It may not have been the ideal manner in which to introduce a student pilot to the spin, but the experience certainly did leave a deep and lasting impression. I approached the spin manoeuvre with a less than enthusiastic attitude for some time.

Since then, I have taken some time to learn about the manoeuvre, to come to a better understanding of exactly what takes place during the event, and to experience quite a number of spins in various aircraft. As a pilot examiner, I have the pleasure of watching commercial pilot candidates spin the aircraft on every check ride.

If I understand how something works, what events will occur during a sequence, and what positive steps I can take to rectify a problem I find I am in a much better position to deal with it effectively.

In a paper presented at the NTSB General Aviation Accident Prevention Symposium, September 21-22, 2000, Rick Stowells writes, "In recent years, stall/spin accidents have accounted for roughly 12% of general aviation accidents but 25% of fatal accidents."

The fact that one in four general aviation fatalities is tied to the stall/spin is certainly an excellent argument for why spin training is still included in pilot training in Canada.

Our friends south the line, in their wisdom, discontinued spin training in 1949 in favour of increased stall training and have hardly looked back since, although a number of specialized schools do provide spin training for those interested in the manoeuvre. And, indeed, the number of stall/spin accidents reported in NTSB accident data since 1949 has decreased, and, having looked at the available data, there does not seem to be a significant difference between the number or severity of stall/spin accidents between the US and Canada, despite Canadian pilot training continuing to include spin training as part of the private and commercial syllabi.

While for many student pilots spin training is perhaps not a highlight of their training schedule, learning how to successfully and skilfully recognize the sequence of events leading up to the spin and how to prevent an inadvertent spin entry can save lives.

So, what exactly happens when we spin an aeroplane?

We cause or allow an aeroplane to spin by allowing or inducing a stall aggravated by yaw. If an aeroplane is not allowed to stall it cannot spin. If it stalls without yaw movement, it cannot spin.

An aerodynamic stall results when a wing exceeds its critical angle of attack, regardless of airspeed or attitude. Normally, in training, we stall an aeroplane at reduced airspeed at something approaching a normal flight attitude, but airspeed and attitude are not the important factors. Angle of attack is.

If an aeroplane is stalled and at the same moment allowed or caused to yaw, the result is entry to an aerodynamic spin. Yaw may be induced in a variety of ways including improper use of rudder, incorrect use of ailerons, failing to compensate for engine torque, or from turbulence. Normally, in training we intentionally and knowingly use rudder "incorrectly" to allow or produce the required yaw for spin entry.

Typically, unintentional spins occur during take-off or landing when rudder is not correctly applied to maintain coordinated flight or during a climbing turn manoeuvre when the aircraft is allowed or caused to stall.

In a level or descending turn, as the wings stall during a yawing movement, the outside wing, the wing opposite the direction of yaw, will be travelling through the air at a slightly faster speed with a slightly lower angle of attack than the inside wing. The inside wing stalls first and loses lift sooner than the outside wing. We experience this as a wing drop and learn during training that corrective steps must be taken quickly to prevent entering a fully developed spin.

In a climbing manoeuvre involving turn and thus yaw, the outside wing has a higher angle of attack and will stall first, producing a spin in the opposite direction of the yawing movement. This is referred to as a departure stall as it typically occurs during the climb-out phase of flight—perhaps in an attempt to clear an obstacle, return to the aerodrome following an engine failure, or demonstrate our advanced piloting skills for the amazed onlookers on the ground. The departure stall/spin can be a very disorienting event, particularly if it comes as a surprise.

In a spin, initially the rate of rotation about the normal axis, yaw, may be quite minimal, but it increases rapidly. This causes the inside wing, in the case of level or descending flight, or the outer wing, in the case of a climb, to become more deeply stalled. The aircraft drops its nose, increases its rate of yaw towards the more deeply stalled wing and begins to lose its forward momentum. Its flight path takes a more and more vertical trajectory, increasing the angle of attack for both wings and the rate of yaw, rotation.

This process—called autorotation—tends to be self-sustaining: the faster the aeroplane rotates about its normal axis the greater the difference in lift produced by the wings. The aeroplane begins to rotate about its normal axis and assume a helical, vertical flight path, causing the details of the ground below to become increasingly clear and the pilot to become increasingly interested.

At the moment of stall, the centre of pressure—the point through which lift acts—after moving forward as we approach the critical angle of attack, moves rapidly aft, causing the nose of the aircraft to pitch downward, further increasing our vertical movement and providing momentum to increase our rate of rotation about the normal axis.

As the aeroplane assumes a more and more vertical flight path, both wings become deeply stalled: their angles of attack increase with the inside wing remaining more deeply stalled than its outside brother or sister, increasing the tendency to autorotation.

In a light training aeroplane, within something like 4 to 6 seconds, approximately the first two or three turns about the normal axis, the machine establishes itself in a fully developed spin. The attitude the aircraft assumes depends on a number of factors including the location of its centre of gravity. The farther forward the centre of gravity the more the aircraft will tend to assume a nose down attitude.

An extreme aft centre of gravity may result in the aeroplane failing to put its nose down sufficiently to allow recovery from the spin. Kids, don't try this at home.

Once established in a fully developed spin, the nose has a tendency to pitch upward and the machine establishes a repeating pattern of yawing, rolling, and pitching as it continues to turn about its normal axis and descend in a helical and vertical flight path.

This fully developed stage of the spin is maintained by a balance between aerodynamic and inertial forces and movements and is a quite stable condition.

The aeroplane continues to yaw about the normal axis as a result of the differential lift produced by the wings: the outside wing is less stalled and produces more lift than the inside wing. The inside wing, having a higher angle of attack, produces more drag, maintaining the autorotation tendency. The aircraft pitches nose up/nose down as a result of the aerodynamic and inertial forces produced by the yawing motion.

Inertial pitching results from the changing rate of rotation about the normal axis. As the nose drops the rotation rate of the aircraft accelerates inducing an increased tendency for the nose to rise, which, in turn, slows the rate of rotation resulting in the nose pitching downward.

If you would like to experience this first hand on the ground try this trick suggested to me by one of my mentors, Bob: stand with your arms loosely at your sides. Begin to spin around, rotate about your "normal axis". You will notice as your rate of rotation increases there is an increasing tendency for your arms to raise themselves — inertial pitch. As your arms rise, you will note increased difficulty in maintaining rate of rotation. The tendency is to slow down the rate of rotation, which then results in your arms returning to your sides.

As the aircraft increases and decreases its rate of rotation through inertial force changes, the differential lift produced by the wings increases and decreases as well, resulting in a rhythmic rolling movement.

So, there we are in a stable condition of rhythmic movements involving pitch, roll, and yaw as we descend in a helical and vertical flight path toward the ground below.

To recover from the spin, it is necessary to upset this stable and interesting condition.

Normally, we choose to achieve recovery through positive control inputs. Most training aircraft are designed to recover on their own if we simply release the pro-spin inputs: full rudder and full elevator. Positive recovery techniques simply accelerate the recovery process, which is normally considered a good thing. It also allows the pilot to feel useful and needed and serves to boost his or her self- confidence.

As interesting as the spin manoeuvre is, we generally do not choose to prolong it any longer than necessary unless we are executing the manoeuvre as a performance for the amazed crowd below. "Look, mom. That aeroplane is falling out of the sky."

Consult your aircraft POH for the recommended technique for spin recovery. Of course, for intentional spins we would choose to use an aircraft that is both approved for spins and in the required condition of weight and balance.

To execute a successful spin recovery, we need to accomplish two things: we must stop the auto rotation and we must break the stall.

For most training aircraft we can use the acronym PARE to remind us of the spin recovery procedure. P is for power; A is for aileron; R is for rudder; E is for elevator. If we have any flaps deployed on entry, we want to retract them immediately after diagnosing spin entry. Flaps reduce our nose down attitude, flatten the spin, make recovery more difficult, and we may easily exceed Vfe on recovery. Leaving flaps deployed may result in structural damage to the machine.

To recover: flaps up; power idle; ailerons neutral; rudder initially full in the opposite direction to the spin then neutral as soon as autorotation stops; simultaneously, reduce elevator input as required to break the stall. We now find ourselves in a power-off dive and can easily recover the aircraft to a normal flight condition.

Spin training is interesting and, at times, quite focusing. If we understand what is happening and why and what we need to know and do about the situation, we can find ourselves much more comfortable about the whole process. The key knowledge and skill-set training is designed to give a pilot recognition of the conditions and symptoms leading up to spin entry and the necessary techniques for preventing those conditions leading to the fully developed spin.

If we can avoid ever experiencing inadvertent spin entry, we will increase our opportunities to participate in flying for a much longer time to come.

NOTES:

(Endnotes)

1 http://www.tc.gc.ca/media/documents/ca-publications/tp13747e.pdf

2 Distance/Altitude = Lift/Drag. The sides of similar, right triangles are always proportional.

3 $L = \frac{1}{2} CLpV^2S$; $D = \frac{1}{2} CDpV2S$. $L/D = CL/CD$, all other factors cancel.

4 The coefficient of drag is equal to the sum of the coefficient for inducted drag (CDI) plus the coefficient of parasite drag (CDP). The CDI changes with angle of attack. The CDP changes with the shape of the aircraft, for example if we deploy flap or landing gear. There is only one angle of attack in any configuration that produces the maximum number for the L/D ratio.

5 $L = \frac{1}{2} CLpV2S$. The variables over which we have control as a pilot are the Coefficient of Lift, CL, which we change be adjusting angle of attack, and the airspeed, V. Air density, p, at any given altitude, and wing surface, S, are fixed.

6 Kershner, William K., The Advanced Pilot's Flight Manual, Iowa State University Press, 1994, page 111.

PART 3: FLIGHT INSTRUCTION

Chapter 3.1

Choosing a Flight School

"I was sold on flying as soon as I had a taste for it."

-John Glenn

A t any given moment in time, several thousand Canadians of all ages are thinking about flight training. They are young, middle aged, and older men and women who, for reasons shared by many of us, feel the lure of the skies, thrill to the sound of an aircraft accelerating down the runway toward flight, and long to feel the resistance of the stick pulled back in climb.

On any given day, several hundred Canadians are exploring the world of flight training, trying as best they can to choose a school that will suit. They are looking for a school that will satisfy their needs and provide them with a positive venue to meet their aviation goals.

According to Glenn Priestley, the Air Transport Association of Canada's (ATAC) Vice President for Fixed-Wing Air Taxi and Flight Training, there are approximately 5000 students enrolled in flight training programs across Canada at any given time. There are 280 accredited flight schools operating in Canada, 44 in BC alone. That translates into a good basis of choice for any potential student.

Choosing the flight school that's right for you is no small decision, and taking the time to complete a proper investigation is an excellent plan. A survey conducted by ATAC and the Department of National Defense found the average cost of obtaining a private pilot licence in Canada, based on a 48 hour, full time program, is $6869.19. The actual cost of a PPL licence-training program can easily be double this figure.

For students embarking on a career program and working toward a commercial pilot licence endorsed for multi-engine and instrument flight, the cost is closer to the $30,000 to $80,000 range. It may be considerably higher, depending on the total educational package.[1]

ATAC has published some very sound advice for prospective flight students and a visit to their website, http://www.atacca.ca, to read the materials on flight training is well worth the few moments it takes. Among their recommendations is a six-step process:

1. Determine your aviation goals;
2. Identify the type of school you wish to attend;
3. Make a list of possible schools;
4. Visit the schools in person;
5. Assess the bottom line costs; and
6. Make a choice.

The key factor in this whole process is finding a school that will be right for you. Just you. You are looking for a school that will meet your needs, a school that will fit your way of doing things. You want to train with people who will work with you to achieve your aviation goals.

There are essentially three types of flight training schools in Canada: college programs; large, flight-centre or flying club type schools; and smaller, independent schools. Each type of school has its advantages and disadvantages. There is no single, right way to earn a pilot's licence any more than there is only one type of person who wants to learn to fly.

College programs are geared primarily to younger men and women focused on a career in aviation who want to complete either a two-year diploma program or a four-year college degree at the same time they complete their flight training. These programs, on the whole, are excellent and provide younger students with an opportunity to build a strong educational base for a career in aviation. The governing body for college and university aviation programs is the Canadian Association of Aviation Colleges (CAAC) and a visit to their website is an excellent place to start a search to review options.[2]

Following the Colgan Air flight 3407 crash on approach into Buffalo, NY, there has been a significant push in the US for legislation to increase the requirements, both academic and flight training, necessary to qualify to occupy a pilot's seat in a commercial airline operation. One of the ideas gaining traction is to require all new commercial, airline pilots to hold a degree from an accredited aviation college or university. Should this idea work its way into legislation in the US, Canada will not be far behind.

For young men and women serious about a career in professional aviation, a university degree or college diploma may soon become mandatory. Certainly, the intense combination of academic and flight training provides young, aspiring commercial pilots a solid foundation on which to build a viable aviation career.

College programs are, on the whole, expensive. For many students, however, loans and grants are available to assist with the high costs. If you are graduating secondary school, have a good academic record, and are determined on a career in aviation, it is well worth investigating the various aviation college programs available across Canada, including the Royal Military College at Kingston, Ontario.

The large flight-centre, flight club type schools are located at most of the major airports across the country. Many of these institutions have been in business for years and embody a collective memory of thousands of students successfully completing pilot programs. The schools tend to be well-run organizations with excellent facilities and well-maintained aircraft.

Because their programs are focused solely on flight training, the costs may be less than an aviation college or university program and may provide many of the same actual opportunities for employment at completion, should a student be working toward a career in aviation. For both the commercial and private pilot student, this may be an excellent venue. Working toward an academic credential at the same time as one earns his or her pilot licences and ratings increases a candidate's credentials and employability in a rapidly changing and increasingly complex work environment.

These large, flight-centre type schools are also training grounds for young instructors, so flight students may well find they are being taught by young men and women who, while under the supervision of experienced instructors, are learning as they go. It is important when visiting and discussing your flight training opportunities at this type of school to find out who, exactly, will be available to instruct you, how much choice you will be able to exercise about who will provide your instruction, whether you will have one main instructor or a series of instructors, and what level of experience they may have.

Instructor turnover at large schools tends to be high and this can affect your training continuity. Many of the instructors working at these types of institutions are in the process of building flight time to qualify them for a move to a professional pilot job in industry.

Independent flight schools are to be found at many smaller airports and aerodromes across the country. While they operate under the same Transport Canada rules and regulations and are inspected by TC base inspectors just as regularly as any other flight schools in Canada, they tend to be a bit more of a mixed bag. They range from outstanding to adequate, depending on a number of factors.

The small schools' strong points are built around the individualized nature of the instructor-student relationship. The level of training available at the smaller schools can be excellent, but it is very important for a potential student to visit the school in person, have a good look at the facilities the aircraft used for training, and speak with the instructor or instructors who will be available to provide training.

Costs may be somewhat lower at a smaller school due to lower overhead. Unfortunately, they may also be quite a bit higher if the school does not provide students with a well-coordinated, well-articulated training program. Costs on a per-hour basis may not provide the real story. Actual cost for completion of a training program is what we really need to know. There is no substitute for a personal visit that gives you a chance to look and check and ask.

The current economic environment has not been kind to smaller flight training units. In 2001, there were 287 flight-training units in Canada providing training toward the commercial pilot licence; currently, there are 207, a decrease of almost 30%. One important factor to consider when choosing a flight school is to assess the school's viability; will they be able to continue to be able to provide well maintained equipment and experienced instructors during the time required for you to obtain the licences or ratings to which you aspire?

For both private and commercial pilot students, the small, independent school can, if it is well organized and well run by professional flight instructors, provide an excellent, personalized venue where training can be tailored to a student's personal needs and goals.

With all schools it is an excellent idea, when you are getting close to a decision, to purchase an introductory flight. It isn't a bad idea to do this at a few schools for comparison. For a very reasonable cost you will have an exciting adventure that may also count towards your total flight time requirements, and you will have an up-close-and-personal opportunity to see what sort of instruction you may be able to expect.

Choosing a flight school that's right for you can be an enjoyable and interesting process. The best advice anyone can give you is this: do your homework. Check out available information, both information provided by the schools themselves and information available on ATAC's website and in various other publications.

Ask people in the industry for their thoughts and recommendations; talk to current and former students at schools you are considering; make personal visits. You're preparing to spend a good deal of money and, possibly even more important, a good deal of time and energy.

Five years from now, as you descend to land at a strange aerodrome through what is beginning to feel suspiciously like very marginal weather, that $50.00 you saved by short cutting your investigations may not seem like such a great bargain.

It's your adventure; make it work for you.

NOTES:

Chapter 3.2

Should I Consider a Flight Instructor Rating?

"Education is not the filling of a pail, but the lighting of a fire."
-William Butler Yeats

In our modern world, we often hear the term *collateral damage* referring to unintended but perhaps necessary consequences to an activity. Less frequently we may come across the idea of *collateral benefit*: an unintended or secondary positive outcome to an activity. The major focus of the flight training industry is to train pilots; a *collateral benefit* to that activity is an opportunity to identify and train pilot trainers, flight instructors.

For many young aspiring pilots, becoming a flight instructor is an excellent way to break into the aviation industry. At the bottom of the commercial aviation food chain, competition for jobs is brisk and a young person wanting to break in must develop experience and knowledge beyond that acquired during basic training toward the commercial pilot licence.

Employers seek candidates who are serious about a career in aviation and have the initiative to dig in and acquire the skills, knowledge, and experience necessary to become a valuable employee.

Earning a flight instructor rating is one way to successfully get a foot in the door of commercial aviation, gain valuable experience, and build the pilot-in-command hours to qualify for a responsible position in the world of flying.

As established instructors, an important part of our job is to recognize and encourage those with the requisite skills, knowledge, and interactional skills involved in flight training to consider earning a flight instructor rating, even if that is only for a limited period of time, one step along the pathway toward a career in aviation.

While earning a flight instructor rating is one excellent way to gain entry to the world of aviation, it is not a path for every aspiring pilot. Many potentially excellent flight instructors will never consider an instructor rating and, so it appears, some candidates who are not well suited to instruction do find themselves working toward the instructor rating.

Each person thinking of becoming a flight instructor should spend some serious time exploring, considering, and thinking about the project before signing up. The real question is not whether earning a flight instructor rating is a good way into aviation; the question is whether earning a flight instructor rating is the right path for a particular individual. As experienced flight instructors, we can offer some excellent insights into the world of flight training and assist potential candidates to evaluate both the profession and their suitability to it.

While I would never say either yes or no to a particular potential candidate, I would certainly consider it worthwhile to ask some of the important questions and share some of the real life experiences around what it means to me to be involved with this industry.

It's one of those good news/bad news stories.

First, the bad news.

There are several reasons to discard the idea of becoming a flight instructor, and it is a good idea to review some of them with potential candidates and encourage them to take those reasons under serious consideration before jumping in with both feet. An artist friend of mine used to be a teacher at the Emily Carr School of Art in Vancouver. He taught painting. He loved art and being an artist, but one of the things he used to say to new students was, "If you have any options [to becoming an artist], take them." Perhaps this is not bad advice for aspiring pilots considering becoming flight instructors.

Earning a flight instructor rating is not an easy project. It's a lot of work. It's expensive. It takes a good deal of time, effort, and focus and, once you have earned the rating, there is no guarantee of a job. If you do find a job teaching flying, you can plan on long hours, low pay, and a learning curve that goes on and on, getting steeper as you go. The challenges just keep on coming.

You will have difficult students. You will have long trying days.

There will certainly be days when a job bagging groceries at Safeway starts to seem like a good option. Flight instruction is not for everyone.

Some employers are not keen on hiring pilots with an instructional background. While a person with instructional experience may have acquired considerable PIC time, he or she will have spent relatively little time actually handling the controls of an aircraft or making decisions about flying in difficult and varying situations. Typically, flight instruction takes place in an area familiar to the instructor in good weather conditions.

Now, for the good news.

On the other side of the coin, earning a flight instructor rating will provide a young pilot with an excellent opportunity to really begin the process of acquiring a deep understanding of the underlying principles of flight. It will provide an opportunity to develop skills for working with a variety of different people with different learning styles and expectations, and it will provide a work environment where "by the book", disciplined flying is a regular and every day event.

Please note the word opportunity. As my brother likes to say, "Education is largely self-inflicted." As a student, once again, it is up to the candidate to make use of the opportunity to learn and develop.

Ideally, a flight instructor will begin his or her aviation career working in a monitored and mentored environment. Good flying practices and good decision-making will be emphasized and acted on for each and every flight. Planning skills will be well developed, and accurate evaluative practices and record keeping will be a normal part of all flight activities. The developing instructor will learn to focus on achieving excellence in performance and clarity of understanding that can be used to assist others learning to be safe and competent pilots.

The flight instructor will learn to make decisions, act on evaluations, and live with the consequences of those decisions. There are few more interesting moments than those experienced by a young instructor sending his or her student for a first solo, a first solo cross country, or a flight test.

Many employers actually prefer to interview candidates with an instructional background. A good record as an instructor demonstrates a potential employee has developed a solid basic understanding of the principles of flight, a willingness to accept responsibility, and a willingness to work within a disciplined and focused aviation environment.

Looking through the recent aviation job ads indicates the number of instructional jobs is increasing. For a number of years following 9/11, aviation stagnated and jobs in the industry were few and far between. Now, however, the aviation industry appears to be expanding; baby boomers are reaching retirement age at a rapid rate. Many employers are increasingly looking to the pool of experienced flight instructors to fill vacancies they are facing. This bodes well for people thinking of earning a flight instructor rating as a way into the field of aviation.

If you are considering the flight instructor route, take some time and make the effort to explore it. Do you enjoy working with people? Do you have some comfort level in helping others? Are you willing and able to work within a focused and disciplined learning environment, and are you committed to improving your skills, understanding, and patience? Are you able and willing to put your own quirks and needs aside sufficiently to work positively with those brought to you by your students?

Flight instruction is not for everyone. It's too hard to do as a punishment or as something to "just get through" on the way to a "better" situation. To become a good flight instructor, a person must gain enjoyment from the process of teaching and learning for what it is and understand that the skills and understanding gained are a priceless benefit.

For the right people, earning a flight instructor rating may be a path worth exploring.

NOTES:

Chapter 3.3

Recency Requirements

"You must continue to practice your skills. You are either formally trained and current or you are unqualified."

-Ann Walco

As a Chief Flight Instructor and operator of a flight school, I speak with a steady stream of pilots wanting to know what they need to do to "get flying again" after an absence from aviation. I had a great conversation a few days back with a man who had earned his Commercial Pilot Licence back in the late 1970s but hadn't been in a light aircraft for the past 18 years. After we returned from a local flight he said, through a great big smile, "I guess you don't ever forget how to fly; you just get a bit rusty around the edges."

Being familiar with recency requirements is a good plan for all of us, even if we think of ourselves as active pilots. It is important to be aware of and to ensure we are meeting the legal requirements to act as pilot-in-command of a Canadian registered aircraft. Many active pilots are quite surprised to find that, despite flying on a regular basis, they do not meet the legal recency requirements as laid down in the Canadian Aviation Regulations (CARs).

CAR 401.05,[3] in its majesty, spells out the requirements to maintain, or regain, our currency. The requirements are specified for time periods of six-months, two years, and five years. The five-year recency requirement has been in place for years; the two-year requirement was introduced with the CARs in October 1996.

To remain current to carry passengers, within six months of a flight a pilot must have completed at least five takeoffs and landings in the same category and class of aircraft he or she will be flying. Night landings and takeoffs satisfy both the day and night requirement. Day takeoffs and landings are valid for flights during daytime only.

IFR recency has its own particular requirements. An instrument rating is valid for a period of 24 months, but 12 months following a flight test, the six-month rules become active. So, within six months preceding an IFR flight, a pilot must have logged at least six hours of instrument time and completed six instrument approaches to Canadian Air Pilot, CAP, minimums.

If you are an aircraft renter, it is important to remember that particular flight schools or other aircraft rental organizations may have their own recency requirements, normally more constraining that those required by the CARs. Our school, for example, requires a 60-day recurrency. Following an initial check out with an instructor, unless you have flown one of our aircraft of the type you intend to fly within the last 60 days, we require a fresh check out. We have several pilots, some very experienced, who will come in once every month or six weeks, take an aircraft up for an hour, enjoy a local flight and some circuits to maintain their currency and proficiency.

The two-year recency requirement that came into effect in 1996 is something, I suspect, many pilots have not fully come to grips with. CARs 401.05(2)(a) lists a number of options for meeting the requirement. A pilot may, for example, complete a flight review with a person holding a flight instructor rating valid for the same category of aircraft that will be flown. A flight review basically covers the same items included on a flight test for the licence held by the pilot. Having satisfactorily completed the flight review, a pilot will have his or her logbook endorsed by the instructor stating that the skill requirements of the licence have been met.

Attendance at a Transport Canada safety seminar with the appropriate logbook endorsement enables a pilot to meet the two-year recency requirement, as well. These seminars, I can say from personal experience, are excellent and, normally, very enjoyable. They even supply donuts and coffee, sometimes. It gives us a chance to meet with other pilots from our area to hear about and discuss safety issues and to be updated on current practices and areas of concern: a very worthwhile activity.

Pilots may also fulfill their two-year recency by completing a recurrent training program designed to update their knowledge of human factors, meteorology, flight planning and navigation, and aviation regulations. Completing and retaining for inspection the self-paced study program provided through the Canada Aviation Safety Newsletter, completing the requirements for a licence renewal or a new rating, or completion of a written exam for a permit, licence or rating will also meet the two-year recency requirements.

Pilots holding an Instrument Rating, will automatically meet the two year requirement, as they are required to complete an IFR flight test every two years to maintain their rating.

To comply with the five-year recency requirement, a pilot must have acted as pilot-in-command or co-pilot of an aircraft requiring a two pilot crew, within the five years preceding the flight. He or she may also, within 12 months preceding the flight, have completed a flight review as described in CARs 421.05, including completion of the appropriate exam.

Pilots who have not acted as PIC or copilot of a two pilot aircraft within a five-year period must successfully re-write the PSTAR exam and complete a flight review with a qualified flight instructor to regain their currency.

Of course, a valid Medical Certificate or Licence Validation Certificate (LCV) is also required. Your pilot licence, unless rescinded by Transport Canada, is valid for life. You may not, however, exercise the privileges of that licence unless you hold a valid LCV and are current.

If you have been away from aviation for a period of time and are thinking about getting back in the air, good for you. There is absolutely nothing in the world like the view from the left seat of an aircraft. Come on in and speak with the CFI or another knowledgeable instructor at your favourite flight school. He or she can review your logs with you and let you know exactly what you will need to do to regain your currency status and start flying again.

NOTES:

Chapter 3.4

Lesson Presentation for Instructors

"Planning is bringing the future into the present so that you can do something about it now."

-Alan Lakein

A s Winnie the Pooh said, "Organizing is what you do before you do something, so that when you do it, it is not all mixed up." Any time you watch someone who is really good at doing something do it, it always looks easy. What you don't see is the hundreds and, perhaps, thousands of hours it took to make something complex look easy. As Malcolm Gladwell wrote in his book, The Outliers,[4] it takes something close to 10,000 hours of time on task to really get a grip, to reach a solid journeyman level of performance.

One of the biggest challenges for new instructors and, to be honest, even for more experienced ones, is getting organized so presenting complex material in a simple, understandable fashion can be accomplished to the benefit of students.

Teaching is not about proving we know more than our students; it's about helping students learn.

As they say, any fool can be complex. It takes real genius to make things simple.

Where do I begin? Where do I stop? How much is too much? How much is not enough? These are the questions we are always asking; they are not simple to answer. Experience helps considerably, but experience is what you tend to get right after you needed it.

Particularly in the early days when we are starting out, we don't need the perfect system. What we need is a system that will get us through until we gain the experience necessary to develop our own personal style and method of delivering lesson material in a satisfactory and successful manner.

We don't need to be perfect; we do need to be good enough to get the job done. The basic professional code is, "Do no harm." If we can be certain of achieving that, we have come a good distance down the road to success.

Aviation has developed an outstanding example on how to proceed in a complex environment fraught with potential hazards that is rapidly being incorporated into many other industries: the checklist.

Checklists can be presented in a variety of formats from simple one, two, three listed directions to complex: if this then that; if that then the other thing; or they can be laid out in graphic form: a flow chart. The decision on how to display information rests on how to make pertinent information as clear, simple, and easily followed as possible. What we are after is successful completion of the project in hand; we want our "helpers" to make things easier and simpler not more complex and difficult.

For something like a lesson plan sequence, either for preparing or presenting, I have come to favour the flow chart display. It is simple and easy to follow and allows for additions and modifications, as required, with minimal effort.

Let's take a quick look at lesson plan presentation. Because it is the milieu in which I operate, I have used Canadian references. I will do my best to translate these into generic terms to reduce confusion. Whatever names we give things, flying is still flying, and aerodynamics do not change across borders. PGI, for example, is simply a short version of Preparatory Ground Instruction: the ground teaching providing necessary information for a particular training flight.

It will be helpful to reference the flow chart below as you read along so you can get the visual image along with the words and thoughts.

The first step is to confirm our materials, our student, and we are ready to proceed. The chances of success are sadly reduced if we dash off into the desert without a proper hat, protective clothing, a canteen of water, a map, and a clear sense of our intended destination. A compass might not be a bad idea, either.

The questions to which we need to hear an affirmative answer are: have we reviewed the materials we will be presenting so we are clear on content, examples, theory, and procedures? We may not have taught this particular lesson for some time, so we may need to brush up on it before we start presenting to our student.

Is the learning area clean, neat, and organized? Do we have the required visual aids and other materials required and are they working properly? A projector with a burned out bulb or a toy aeroplane with a broken wing can be less than helpful if they are required to present the lesson.

Once the student has arrived, is he or she physically, mentally, and emotionally ready for this new and exciting adventure? If she, for example, just had a fight with her mother or broke up with her boyfriend the night before, she may not be sufficiently focused to proceed. Did he or she complete any assigned homework or other necessary preparations?

If failure to be prepared is a one-time event, there may be some issues around the specifics of the assignment. If failure to be prepared is part of an ongoing pattern, we may need to have a discussion about responsibilities and commitment.

Now, we're ready to begin the lesson. Everyone comfortable?

Let's provide an overview: "Today, we are going to learn about...." This helps both the student and the instructor focus on the specifics of today's lesson. Keep this short and to the point.

Next, let's review some high points from the previous lesson that will carry through into the current topics, answer any questions the student may have from the last lesson, and go through any assigned homework or other preparations we expect him or her to have completed.

For example, if today's lesson will focus on stalls, it would be an excellent plan to ask a question or two about controlling the aircraft at low airspeeds, slow flight, safe altitudes for manoeuvre training, transfer of control, and how we maintain a good lookout to ensure safety.

Now, let's provide the student with a good overview of today's lesson with emphasis on any specific objective and goals. By the end of today's lesson, for example, we would like you to be able to adjust power and pitch to achieve flight at specific assigned airspeeds while maintaining altitude, heading, and coordinated flight.

Essential Background Knowledge (EBK) is the theory behind today's lesson. Sticking with my previous example, if we are adjusting airspeed we might want to review the relationship between airspeed and angle of attack in terms of maintaining constant lift, the changing dynamics of power, propeller slipstream, propeller angle in relation to flight path, and use of rudder to counter adverse yaw.

Safety is always important, and any specific issues involved with today's flight should be highlighted.

It is always a good plan to provide specific procedures for executing any manoeuvres we plan to work with during the air portion of the lesson. If students learn to be procedural right from the earliest days of their training it will hold them in good stead throughout the complex and sometimes challenging process of learning to fly an aeroplane.

Reviewing what was covered—emphasizing the critical points of the lesson—brings it all into the present and sets the stage for proceeding to flight. Last learned—best remembered: the learning factor of recency.

Answer questions. I always find it helpful to encourage student questions and to make sure there is a place and time for any questions that may come up. If a student finds him or herself pondering something, it takes their attention away from the lesson and impedes their ability to proceed with anything new.

If you have homework or an assignment for the next lesson, give it to the student at the end.

Let's go flying.

Below is an example of a flow chart/checklist for presenting a preparatory ground instruction lesson.

Laying out the steps to follow toward a successful conclusion simplifies the process and lightens the workload. To paraphrase Winnie the Pooh, it's the getting organized part. Having a clearly laid out sequence of events to follow keeps us on track and, if the presentation sequence is shared with students, it allows them to know what information is being presented and anticipate what is coming up next.

When we execute an air manoeuvre we always use the same sequence: safety, set-up, entry, recognition/maintenance and recovery. If we use a similar system for ground lesson presentations, it charts a more easily followed path for students and enables rather than hinders their learning process.

Keeping things simple and straightforward takes much of the guesswork out of the process and both facilitates instructor activities and enhances student learning.

Lesson Plan Presentation checklist

I. Overview

"Today we are going to learn about...."

II. Review (Threshold Knowledge Test)

1. Check Homework Complete
2. Answer Any Questions from previous lesson
3. Review Critical Aspects of Previous Lesson

III. Lesson

1. Objectives of Today's Lesson
2. Theory (Essential Background Knowledge)
3. Considerations and Safety
4. Procedures
5. Review
6. Questions?

IV. Finish and Wrap Up

1. Assign Homework

V. You are Done

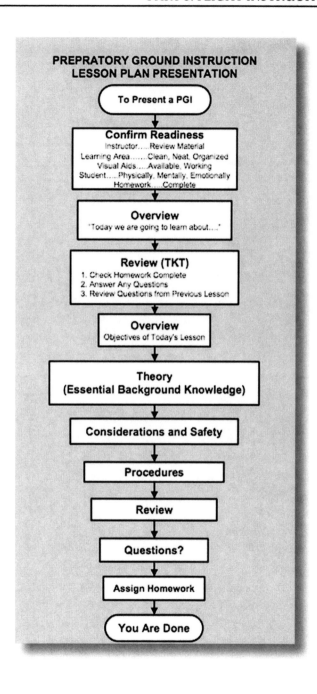

NOTES:

Chapter 3.5

The Flight Instructor/Student Relationship

"We cannot expect a bamboo to grow in a field of reeds."
                                        -Taekwon-Do saying

The flight instructor, his or her student, and the relationship between the two are the essential human cornerstones of the flight training process. All three elements in the equation — teacher, student, and relationship — must be functioning in a satisfactory manner for the process to be successful.

In any working situation, each participant will have responsibilities and roles to fill. It is important to know, if we are to be an active participant and contribute in a positive way to the success of the enterprise, what those responsibilities are and of what the roles consist.

According to a recent American Owners and Pilots Association (AOPA) brochure, "A good flight instructor is an essential component of good primary flight training. And good primary flight training lays the foundation for a lifetime of safe, skilful flying, and learning." I suspect we knew this already, but it can't hurt to remind ourselves, can it?

A good flight instructor can accomplish very little, however, without his or her complements: a good flight student and a positive working relationship.

According to the Transport Canada Flight Instructor Guide, "...for the information and guidance of pilots preparing to apply for flight instructor ratings, and for use as a reference by qualified flight instructors," while acting as a flight instructor, "...your aim is to give students good instruction and sufficient practice so that they can fly aircraft proficiently and safely." [5]

This gives us the basic journeyman definition of the flight instructor's job. It's the equivalent of the "Do no harm" credo of any professional endeavour. The very least we expect is that, at the end of a lesson or succession of lessons, the student will have been told no serious lies and an environment will have been created where learning was possible.

We can, of course, hope for a bit more. We can hope the instructor is well versed in the knowledge, skills and experience of both teaching and flying and is able to create and maintain an excellent learning environment.

We can hope for, as so delightfully described in a Taekwon-Do training manual someone left in my office, for an instructor who demonstrates:

- Strong moral and ethical standards;
- Clear outlook and philosophy in life;
- Responsible attitude as an instructor; and
- Scientific mind in matters of technique.

We can hope for a person who is skilled, knowledgeable, and experienced in both flying and teaching. A proficient pilot with no teaching skills or experience can be just as poor a choice as an instructor as can the person who is a good teacher but lacks the knowledge and skills provided by a depth of experience as a pilot.

Unfortunately, as Ralph Butcher, a very experienced pilot, flight instructor, and contributor to the AOPA magazine 'Flight Training' wrote, "Not all training is equal." Flight training has traditionally been an aviation entry-level job and is often seen as a means for young pilots to earn sufficient PIC hours to qualify for a "real" job in aviation.

Part one of the equation: the flight instructor. Students - check out who will be teaching you, what his or her experience is as a teacher, instructor, and pilot, and how successful he or she has been as a flight instructor in preparing students for successful entry into the world of aviation.

The best instructor in the world, however, can do little to help a student who is not willing or able to deal with the knowledge and skills required to become a pilot. As the Flight Instructor Guide says, "No one ever learns except through their own activity and there is, strictly speaking, no such art as teaching, only the art of helping people learn."

As my brother puts it, "Education is largely self-inflicted."

It is not expected that a student begin flight training with prior knowledge or skills directly related to flying an aircraft. What a student brings to the adventure is a willingness to learn, a decision and a commitment to do the best he or she can, a basic background of knowledge and information including mathematics, physics, language, and a reasonably balanced personality that will be able to sustain the ups and downs, the triumphs and disappointments, of learning to fly.

As the Taekwon-Do manual says, "A student must never tire of learning. A student must always be eager to learn and ask questions."

Active participation and focus on the part of a student is just as important as the information, experience, and positive learning environment created by the instructor.

Part two of the equation: students - have a clear look at your level of commitment to the process of learning to fly and monitor throughout the process your level of effort and focus. If you find yourself in a passive role in the learning process, you will also find your progress very slow and difficult.

Instructors - monitor and inform your students about their level of focus and willingness to participate and contribute to the process. Be willing to discuss this issue if it appears to hinder a student's progress toward the goal of becoming a pilot.

Part three of the equation: the relationship between an instructor and his or her student. We can envision a situation that includes a very good instructor, a very good student, and yet lacks a positive working relationship between the two people. We clearly have a circumstance that will stand in the way of the end goal: the student's progress toward becoming a pilot.

We all have a feel for the basic chemistry between people and are aware of it. In many cases, a little work can clear up differences and open the way to developing the positive working relationship we require. Respect, honesty, integrity, and trust: all excellent descriptors of a successful working relationship.

Sometimes, sadly, it simply isn't going to work, and we need to investigate alternatives.

Students - trust your own sense of how you are being treated. Does your instructor treat you with respect? Is he or she honest, forthright, and forthcoming with the information, both technical and personal, you need to make your training successful? Are you open and honest with your instructor? Are you willing and able to let him or her know when you don't understand or when you feel you may need more or less practice with a concept or skill? Do you have a feeling of trust for your instructor?

Instructors - does your student relate to you with respect and trust? Is he or she able to state his or her concerns? Do you see your student as an important person deserving of your time, energy, and focus as a teacher? Is your student making reasonable and positive progress as a result of what you are doing in the learning environment?

In the field of education, the statement, "I taught her but she didn't learn," is directly equivalent to a doctor saying, "I cured him but he died." The educational process is not about what one person or another does; it is about what everyone involved in the process does and how those activities impact the outcome.

Unless learning is taking place, we do not have a learning environment. We simply have activity.

Working with people is always a complex multi-dimensional endeavour. Whatever role you may currently fill will have its unique set of responsibilities, duties, joys, and challenges. Today's student may be tomorrow's teacher just as today's instructor will most likely be looking for advanced training in the future and will thus become a learner, again.

We describe the pilot licence as a "licence to learn" and, as most experienced pilots will be happy to tell you, aviation is a life-long learning process. From the very beginnings of our aviation careers, it is useful and productive to understand and appreciate the roles, responsibilities, and challenges of, as we might say, both sides and the centre of the coin: the student, the instructor, and the relationship between the two.

NOTES:

Chapter 3.6

Teaching Accelerate Stop Distance

"Only those who will risk going too far can possibly find out how far one can go."

-T.S. Eliot

During basic flight training, we teach students numerous bits and pieces of the art and science of piloting a flying machine. Many of these bits and pieces are retained and, as students move on as pilots gaining experience and, perhaps, continuing their training, they begin to see how some of those bits and pieces begin to coalesce into a coherent picture. The dots begin to connect. Developing pilots learn there are real world applications for the concepts developed during basic training.

As a Pilot Examiner, I have been afforded a valuable window on the progress of aspiring pilots at various stages in their development as they piece together the world of aviation.

One of the very interesting application problems that comes up quite often on flight tests emerges out of a series of questions around takeoff and landing distance calculations. Most students on flight test can produce reasonably accurate calculations of takeoff and landing distances, factoring in the real time wind and runway conditions. Not all, but most. The interesting part tends to emerge when I ask whether or not the licence candidate would feel comfortable using a particular airport or aerodrome for operations, particularly if I ask that question right after a discussion on landing distance requirements.

For almost all small aircraft used in training, the landing distance is approximately half the takeoff distance required under the same conditions. Just because an aircraft can be put down in a given length of runway or landing surface does not mean the machine can be returned to the air from that same landing surface. This reality came as a surprise to at least one person I know after he safely landed his Cherokee Warrior on an 800' grass farm strip.

Taking one more baby step forward, I might ask a licence candidate, "What is the shortest runway from which you would feel comfortable operating given today's conditions?"

I might continue with, "If your aeroplane requires 1200' to achieve flight, would you be comfortable operating from a 1300' takeoff surface?"

Remember, we're talking about normal operations here, not delivering vaccine to dying children.

Unfortunately, for us as pilots, whatever our experience level might be, I don't think anyone has yet developed an "app" that can answer the question, "Is this safe enough?" We all have our own personal *risk tolerance level*. As we move up into larger and more complex aircraft and operations, much of that decision-making is taken away from us, because companies who actually carry the long term effects of risk are not willing to exceed certain defined levels of risk. They achieve this lowered risk level by reducing the discretionary decision-making of their line pilots.

Airline and military operations are prime examples of this process, and their reduced accident/incident rates support the effectiveness of their proactive approach. The stats clearly show that general aviation flight is considerably more prone to accidents and incidents than airline flight. General Aviation accounts for approximately forty times more accidents and incidents per flying hour than do commercial or military flying.

So, what are the factors that limit use of a runway or takeoff surface?

Remember the little acronym we all learned at about 12-15 hours of flight training: OWLSS? The five effective limiting factors when judging whether or not a takeoff and landing surface is useable are: Obstacles, Wind, Length, Surface and Slope. Those are the factors; however, the real question is against which standard do we evaluate? Just because the aircraft's POH or AFM says the machine is capable of landing or taking off in a given distance in given conditions does not mean that distance is our only limitation or that our risk tolerance level is being met.

We can only imagine how the first person to discover the concept of Accelerate Stop Distance (ASD) came by his or her realization. If it was accomplished the way the majority of new realizations are achieved in aviation, I suspect it involved a pile of wreckage that had come to a stop somewhat past the available takeoff surface shortly after the engine noise abruptly diminished.

While Accelerate Stop Distance is a term we do not normally encounter until we start flying multi engine aircraft, it is a very useful concept to work with even with smaller single engine machines. It is an excellent tool for helping students, instructors, and all of us manage risk.

We simply cannot achieve perfect safety in aviation or anywhere else on this planet, but we can be aware of potential hazards and start teaching students early in their training process ways to manage the level of risk we, and they, choose to accept while involved in a particular endeavour.

Accelerate Stop Distance is the distance required for an aeroplane on takeoff to accelerate from stand-still to flying speed, encounter a problem, have the pilot realize and accept there is a problem, close the throttles, apply the brakes, and stop on the runway or takeoff surface available.

Larger aircraft AFMs provide ASD information in the form of tables or charts, enabling pilots to easily and quickly evaluate the usability of a particular takeoff surface under particular conditions. For light aircraft, ASD is not normally provided by the manufacturer, but we can make some fairly useful estimates if we analyze the component parts. This can be both a useful and interesting challenge for student pilots working toward understanding the hows and whys of aviation and risk management.

The first part is easy: how much distance do we need to get from a standing start to flying speed?

Most light aircraft POHs will provide that information in the form of a takeoff distance chart or graph. Some—the Aeronca Champion and the J3 Cub come to mind—do not. For aircraft that only provide distance for short field takeoff, it might be an excellent plan to add a safety margin for a normal takeoff—what we normally would use—of perhaps 15%.

The second part, the distance required to notice a problem and respond, is a bit harder to work with. Some of us are quicker and less afflicted with denial than others. At sixty knots we cover approximately 100′ every second. For the average training aircraft with the average pilot, perhaps 300-400 feet would be a reasonable reaction time in the event of a malfunction.

Sometimes, empirical data is the best we can do. Pick a nice, long runway and tell your student you will announce an engine failure on the takeoff run. See how long it takes him or her to respond.

For the third component, the one after the throttle is closed and the brakes are applied, we can refer to the POH's landing distance charts.

Adding the three components together we can come to a reasonable approximation of the distance required to ensure the risk of running off the takeoff surface in the event of an engine failure is minimized. Note: I used the word *minimized* rather than the word *eliminated*. What we are doing is reducing and managing risk not eliminating it. This is a very salient point to make with students: our goal is to minimize risk and keep it within our risk tolerance parameters rather than eliminate it.

What we are doing during this process is developing a tool to help us evaluate the level of risk we are willing to accept when deciding to make use of a particular runway surface to achieve the miracle of flight.

For one example, under no wind conditions at 3000' pressure altitude and 20^0 C, according to the POH a fully loaded C-172P will become airborne in 1230'. Using my makeshift system for calculating, that same machine would require approximately 2145' to accommodate a reasonable ASD. A reasonable minimum takeoff run available (TORA) might start looking a lot more like 2500' rather than, say, 1500'.

The chances of having an actual engine failure on takeoff in a well maintained modern aircraft are slight. That is good news. As the stats tell us, a very small percentage of accidents, approximately 15%, result from machine failure. As a friend of mine often says, it is the weak link between the stick and the rudder pedals that causes all the problems.

Taking into account potential known risk factors and taking positive steps to mitigate their risk to an acceptable level is always a reasonable decision, and the process of evaluating risk level is an important tool students can take away as one of the "bits and pieces" they retain from basic flight training.

Below is a sample ASD chart developed around the takeoff performance numbers for the C-172M. It is for training purposes only and does not predict actual performance nor is it a product of the manufacturer.

ACCELERATE STOP DISTANCE C-172P

-- This chart is to be used for training purposes only --

CONDITIONS:
- Flaps up
- Full Power on Takeoff Roll
- Throttles Closed at Engine Failure
- Maximum Braking During Deceleration
- Paved, Level, Dry Runway
- Zero Wind

Notes:

1. Decrease distances by 10% for each 9 knots headwind.
2. For operation with tailwinds up to 10 knots, increase distances by 10% for each 2 knots.
3. For operation on dry grass runways, increase distances by 15% of the normal takeoff distance plus 45% of the short field ground roll figure adjusted for wind as per the aircraft POH

SAMPLE ACCELERATE – STOP DISTANCE TABLE C-172M

This chart is to be used for training purposes only

Weight in Pounds	Takeoff Speed KIAS	Pressure Altitude in Feet	ACCELERATE – STOP DISTANCE IN FEET				
			0⁰C	10⁰C	20⁰C	30⁰C	40⁰C
2300	55	S.L	1605	1690	1775	1865	1950
		1000	1705	1790	1885	1980	2080
		2000	1810	1905	2005	2110	2220
		3000	1925	2030	2145	2260	2380
		4000	2060	2175	2290	2425	2555
		5000	2200	2330	2460	2605	2750
		6000	2365	2500	2650	2810	2970
		7000	2545	2700	2860	3035	-----
		8000	2745	2920	3100	-----	-----

This chart is to be used for training purposes only

NOTE: Cessna does not choose to provide an Accelerate Stop Distance (ASD) chart for the C-172. The sample ASD chart has been constructed for training purposes only at ABC Flight School. The calculations for the chart are based on normal takeoff distances plus a 300 foot allowance for reaction time in the event of an abnormality on takeoff plus a distance equal to the short field landing distance as provided in the aircraft POH.

The chart provides a reasonable estimation of the **minimum** distance required to accelerate to 55 KIAS then stop in an emergency. A rejected takeoff is, however, a very difficult manoeuvre for pilots to complete within specified distances. Accident statistics show that pilots often take longer to react in an emergency than ASD charts allow for and then often do not apply maximum braking initially. It is critical that pilots realize in the event of an abnormality, if they reject takeoff, they will only achieve the distance specified in an ASD chart if they promptly reduce power to idle and apply maximum braking immediately. It is the pilot's responsibility to ensure that actual conditions are considered and that an aircraft is operated in a safe manner.

Accelerate Stop Distance can also easily be represented in a graph form. We have developed an interactive graph that allows students to input density altitude, aircraft weight, and wind and generate an accelerate stop distance.[6]

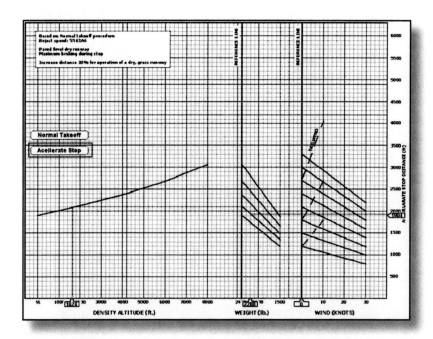

Chapter 3.7

Tail Draggers

"I fly because it releases my mind from the tyranny of petty things."
-Antoine de Saint-Exupery

For many years, the thought of learning to fly on an airplane with its third wheel located at the back has been discounted in mainstream aviation training. The infamous "taildragger", the conventional gear aircraft, has come to represent a throwback to times past and gone. They're too hard to fly; you'll ground loop; you'll end up upside down and backward.

"Modern" aircraft are configured with the tricycle gear, third wheel in the front configuration: what the Cessna Aircraft Corporation referred to as, "Land-O-Matic" landing gear when they introduced the C-150 trainer.

In the last few years, however, more and more people have re-visited the idea of learning to fly on a tail wheel aircraft, and a number of flight schools across Canada and in the United States have begun to offer basic, advanced, and transition instruction on these interesting and delightful machines.

There was a time, not too far in the past, when every aspiring pilot learned to fly on a conventional gear aircraft as a matter of course. Small training aircraft were built that way, and even larger aircraft, including passenger and transport aircraft, were so configured. Hence the term: "conventional gear".

Since the 1950s, we have come to consider the tricycle gear as the "normal" configuration for an aircraft and have almost ceased to give the topic further consideration. There is, however, a good argument for the continued use of conventional gear aircraft for basic training, and it is worth considering it as a serious option when making decisions at the beginning of a flying career or along the way as an added capability and skill set.

The argument goes something like this: training on a taildragger makes you a better pilot. Now, that is a broad statement and could probably use some level of shading if it to carry any serious weight, but there is some truth in it.

The key difference between the conventional gear or taildragger aircraft and modern tricycle gear aircraft is the location of the centre of gravity in relation to the location of the main landing gear wheels. In a tricycle gear aircraft, the centre of gravity is located ahead of the main gear; in a conventional gear aircraft, the centre of gravity is located aft of the main gear.

Why is this so important a difference? Simply put, the centre of gravity of an object—its centre of mass—has a positive tendency to lead, to move to the front of the machine's direction of travel. That's why an arrow arrives at its target head first, why a weighted stick will always arrives back on the surface of the planet weighted end down, or why we install mass balance weights in the leading edge of rudders, elevators, and ailerons.

With a tricycle gear aircraft, as it taxies down the runway, touches down on landing, or lifts itself into the air, the centre of gravity assists the aircraft to track straight. This simplifies the pilot's efforts to achieve simple and easy manoeuvring. It also allows a lower level of perfection in use of the rudder, elevator, and aileron controls. The aircraft does more of the work and allows the pilot to achieve safe ground handling and flight with a lower level of skill. If the pilot gets a bit sloppy on his or her controls, the aircraft will, most of the time, bail the pilot out of the potential mess.

Certainly, this is a very strong argument in favour of the tricycle gear configuration and one not to be depreciated in any way. It's one of the significant reasons why tricycle gear aircraft have dominated the aviation scene and will continue to do so unless or until some bright soul comes up with a better idea.

Tail draggers, on the other hand, require a higher level of skill to achieve safe ground handling, take-offs, and landings. that is the core argument for the use of conventional gear aircraft in training. The pilot must develop a higher skill level in aircraft control to achieve safe ground handling and flight. He or she must become very proficient in fine control. The consequences of lack of skill are immediate, embarrassing, and sometimes worse.

The bottom line is that no ground manoeuvre, take-off, or landing with a conventional gear aircraft can be taken for granted. The machine is "in flight" from the moment you cast off the tie-down ropes until you have them, once again, firmly tied at the end of the flight. You, as pilot, must be in control. Rather than help you out, the machine has a built-in tendency to end up backwards, given any opportunity.

So, why in the world would a person consider taking flight training on a conventional gear aircraft? Simply this: you will develop those critical aircraft handling skills — use of rudder, aileron, and elevator — to a high level of proficiency. You will, as a pilot, have learned and earned a high level of confidence in your abilities to handle an aircraft as a product of your training and experience. You will emerge from your training more skilled, more focused, and better qualified as a stick and rudder airplane driver.

Besides, it just about the most fun you can have and still keep your pants on.

The Fleet 80, better known as the Fleet "Canuck."
Perhaps, the best light training aircraft ever built.

Chapter 3.8

Instrument Flight

"I have never been to Pulo Prabang alas, but I understand it possesses all the advantages of Borneo without the drawback of head-hunters."

-Patrick O'Brien

Accroding to the American Owners and Pilots Association, "Attempting VFR flight in instrument meteorological (IMC) conditions is one of the most consistently lethal mistakes in all of aviation. Since 2002, more than 86% of all fixed-wing VFR-into-IMC accidents have been fatal, a higher proportion than for mid-air collisions, wire strikes, or pilot incapacitation."

The National Transportation Safety Board in the US has stated clearly, "VFR flight into instrument meteorological conditions (IMC) is still one of the leading causes of fatal GA accidents."

As James Marasa wrote in his excellent article, VFR in IMC: Why Good Pilots fly in Bad Weather,[7] "...practically speaking, no other type of accident is responsible for claiming more lives than pilots unintentionally flying a mechanically sound aircraft into the ground."

Under current regulations, candidates for the Canadian Private Pilot Licence (Aeroplane) are required to receive a minimum of five hours instrument flight training. Up to three of those hours may be completed on an approved flight simulator. The licence candidate is also required to demonstrate some degree of proficiency with instrument flight on his or her flight test and some very basic level of knowledge on his or her written exam. Two flight test exercises are focused on this activity. The licence candidate must demonstrate straight and level flight for two minutes, a 180 degree rate one turn, followed by two more minutes straight and level flight, and he or she must demonstrate recovery from one unusual attitude.

For many general aviation pilots, their basic training may be the last time they experience instrument flight unless they continue their training by earning a night, VFR over the top, or instrument rating. As we all know, skills left lying dormant do not improve with time.

Sadly, humans seem to have an undying belief that if we can perform an activity to a reasonable level of proficiency at one time, that level of proficiency is guaranteed for life.

During pilot training, instructors attempt to provide aspiring pilots, during their five hours of instrument flight training, with the basic skills to extract themselves from an inadvertent encounter with non-VFR conditions. Training pilots to have the judgement to avoid IMC is often more complex and involves a life-long commitment to safe piloting practices.

As an instructor, I've heard many, many times students saying, "But I'll never do that." And yet, every year VFR pilots are seriously injured or killed as a result of losing control of their aircraft as a direct result of spatial disorientation caused by flight into IMC conditions.

National Transportation Safety Board (NTSB) statistics show attempted VFR flight into IMC account for a significant portion of the total number of accidents resulting from spatial disorientation.

According to the AOPA Air Safety Foundation, "The US Aeronautical Information Manual ranks spatial disorientation among the most cited contributing factors to fatal accidents. From 1994 through 2003, it caused at least 202 accidents [in the United States]. One hundred eighty-four of them involved fatalities."

The following is a part of the synopsis prepared by the Transportation Safety Board of Canada (TSB), Final Report A98A0184:

> "Spatial disorientation occurs when a pilot's sense or "orientation percept" of the position, motion, or attitude of his/her aircraft or himself/herself with respect to the earth's surface and the gravitational vertical is based on incorrect or misinterpreted sensory information. Pilots with limited instrument flight time are most susceptible to spatial disorientation.
>
> "Knowledge and experience are the key determinants of a pilot's susceptibility to disorientation. A pilot's only defense against spatial disorientation is to develop the ability to suppress natural vestibular responses through training and practice (vestibular suppression), and to always use visual information from the instruments to maintain spatial orientation (instrument discipline) and, consequently, his/her situational awareness."

Having an instrument rating is only part of the remedy, however. In nearly half (47%) of VFR-into-IMC accidents reviewed in NTSB data, the pilot was instrument rated.

Trained does not mean qualified. An excellent example of a Controlled Flight Into Terrain is described in the TSB accident report A08P0353, in a highly trained, very experienced commercial pilot flew his Grumman G-21A into the hill on South Thormanby Island, BC.[8] I remember the day of this accident well. As Chief Flight Instructor at a flight-training unit not far from the crash site, I had grounded all our aircraft due to the poor weather conditions prevailing.

As Ann Walco, a commercial pilot, flight instructor, and FBO manager so clearly put it, "You must continue to practice your skills. You are either formally trained and current or you are unqualified."

As most of us have learned, a little knowledge can be a dangerous thing. It is certainly possible to know just enough to give us the confidence get into serious trouble without possessing sufficient depth of knowledge or skill to get us back out.

Taking a bit of time to get some re-currency training on instruments and to review the situations that can lead to inadvertent entry into IMC is an excellent plan, even if you may never intend to make use of those skills. Most VFR pilots avoid flying into IMC conditions like the plague. But, and this is the big but, it does happen. You can inadvertently or as a result of poor decision-making find yourself in a situation where visual reference is lost or very uncertain. This is not a moment to be relying on skills learned years ago and never practiced.

You can think of it in the same light as practicing emergency procedures or taking a jacket with you on a sunny day. Being ready for an event you hope will never occur may be your best insurance against it actually coming to pass.

You may also be very pleased with the way a bit of additional instrument training will fine-tune the rest of your flying.

If we can manage to remove some of the "head-hunters" from a potentially dangerous situation by being well trained and current with the necessary skills and knowledge, it can substantially reduce the odds we will become one of the sad statistics compiled by the TSB and the NTSB regarding spatial disorientation events.

Learning is, after all, a life-long adventure.

NOTES:

Chapter 3.9

Integrating Crew Briefings into Basic Training

"Begin at the beginning," the King said gravely, "and go till you come to the end; then stop."

-Lewis Carroll

In the multi-crew environment of commercial aviation, standard procedures require pilots to participate in thorough crew briefings as part of their preparation for manoeuvres. The briefings serve at least three important functions: they let the pilots hear and understand exactly what manoeuvre will be performed; they specify who will do what when; and they allow the pilots an opportunity to be assured agreement exists on the procedures to be carried out and what the plan includes for contingencies.

There is a fourth and also important aspect to verbal briefings: they bring the plan into tangible form that allows review and scrutiny. They lay it out so it can be seen, felt, and understood, step by step.

A verbal briefing serves much the same purpose as reaching out to touch an instrument or gauge when confirming function or taking a reading. The action of touching helps make the check real.

The act of speaking and/or hearing a briefing helps make the plan real.

of the major keys to aviation safety and reliability is redundancy. If you need one, let's put two on board. If two is good and we have room, let's have three, just in case.

In the August *2011* issue of Psychological Science, a journal of the Association for Psychological Science, a Dutch team of scientists reported they were able to confirm for the first time that speaking and understanding speech share the same functional parts of the brain.[9] The act of speaking allows both the speaker and the listener an opportunity to doubly exercise the part of the brain involved in understanding.

Clarity and understanding are critical in order to carry out a plan successfully. Verbalizing and laying out a plan of action also serves as a form of "mental simulation" allowing decision-makers to act out in their minds the up-coming actions again, step by step. Research demonstrates this process allows decision makers to focus on critical cues, identify causal factors, and reduce the information overload that may occur during complex activities.[10]

According to the most recent Canadian Transportation Safety Board's (TSB) yearly summary report of aviation accidents in Canada (2010), general aviation flying continues to show the highest rate of accidents and fatalities for any category of flight activity. In 2010, out of a total 244 aviation accidents, private pilots accounted for 147, 60% of the total number of aviation accidents in Canada.

According to the US National Transportation Safety Board (NTSB), "Each year, hundreds of people — 450 in 2010 — are killed in GA accidents, and thousands more are injured. GA continues to have the highest aviation accident rates within civil aviation: about 6 times higher than small commuter and air taxi operations and over 40 times higher than larger transport category operations.[11]

In terms of accident statistics, the most critical phases of flight occur during takeoff, approach, and landing. TSB statistics show these three phases of flight accounted for 71% of all aviation accidents involving aeroplanes for the year 2010.[12]

of the crucial differences between private and commercial flying is the consistent use of well thought-out and tested standard operating procedures (SOPs) in commercial operations.

While the majority of people working toward a Private Pilot Licence may not have an interest in moving farther toward the world of commercial flight, adopting some of the more successful aspects of that world can be very helpful in increasing the safety margin under which they fly.

For those students who do plan to continue their flight training to more advanced levels, getting started on the right foot with at least a basic grounding in the concept of procedural flying is an excellent plan.

Integrating the use of crew briefings prior to critical manoeuvres such as takeoff, approach, and landing is an easy step to move the ball toward the goal of reducing accidents and incidents in the general aviation community.

If we establish and articulate a clear plan of action, including contingency planning, prior to initiating a manoeuvre, we stand a much better chance of successfully completing that manoeuvre, and, in the event of an unforeseen difficulty, dealing successfully with that contingency.

A simple, pre-takeoff crew briefing on a checklist might look something like this:

Pre-Takeoff Crew Briefing

This will be a (Normal/Short/Soft) Takeoff Rwy ___
Runway conditions are: ___
Winds are: ___
Go/No Go point will be: ___

Lining Up I Will Confirm:
Compass/HI ...... CONFIRM RUNWAY HEADING
Runway .... CLEAR

On Takeoff Roll I Will Confirm:
Throttle .... FULL
RPM .... STATIC POWER (Minimum)
Gauges .... GREEN
Airspeed .... ALIVE
Rotate .... _____ Knots
Climb Out ...... _____ Knots

Any Malfunction Prior To Lift Off I Will:
Call .... "REJECT"
Throttle ..... IDLE
Brakes ...... APPLY
Flaps .... RETRACT

Engine Failure After Takeoff (No Runway Remaining)
Carb Heat .... HOT
Set _____ Knots Glide
Land .... STRAIGHT AHEAD
 (Manoeuvring only to avoid obstacles)

If Time, Shut Down:
Mixture .... IDLE CUTOFF
Fuel .... OFF
Mags .... OFF
Flaps .... SET
Master .... OFF
Passengers .... BRIEF

As Winnie the Pooh said, "Organizing is what you do before you do something, so that when you do it, it is not all mixed up."

Incorporating simple yet thorough crew briefings as part of checklist procedures prior to critical manoeuvres is an excellent way for students to ensure they have a clear plan, a procedure including contingency planning, to follow. It provides an excellent, simple, foundational step, particularly for less experienced pilots to help ensure a positive outcome during the most critical phases of flight.

NOTES:

Chapter 3.10

Establishing and Maintaining Quality Assurance

"Quality is never an accident; it is the result of high intention, sincere effort, intelligent direction and skilful execution; it represents the wise choice of many alternatives."

-William A. Foster

There has been considerable discussion recently regarding the state of flight training in North America and what we as instructors and professional aviation educators can do to improve and maintain this important industry.

In the US, the Society of Aviation and Flight Educators (SAFE) held a seminar in early May 2011 to develop a set of positive recommendations for improvement in flight training. They produced a list of more than 20 specific changes, ranging from improvements in training doctrine, higher standards for instructor refresher courses, better guidance for flight reviews, scenario-based risk management training, and a closer look at how simulators of various types might be put to better use in training new pilots and keeping existing certificate holders sharper and safer.

As a result of a Congressional mandate, FAA administrator Randy Babbitt issued a press release detailing what he calls, "... the most significant changes to air carrier training in 20 years.... a major effort to strengthen the performance of pilots... through better training."

The Canadian Aviation Maintenance Council (CAMC) in partnership with the Air Transport Association of Canada (ATAC) recently completed and released an update to the 2010 Human Resource Study of the Commercial Pilot in Canada[13] that highlights some valuable information for all of us involved in pilot training.

One of the key ways to assist us in achieving quality operations and instruction is to clearly define what quality actually looks like, smells like, tastes like, and means in the various specific activities that make up our training programs. Without clearly defined, articulated, and measurable standards there is little opportunity for us to consciously produce continual improvement and ensure success.

Setting ourselves up to achieve ongoing improvement can be seen as a three-step process:

1. Describe and Articulate Quality Targets;
2. Implement a data driven decision-making process; and
3. Implement a Quality Audit System.

Unless can clearly define what quality is and how we can recognize it, our chances of achieving it are slight. Unless you know where you are going, your chances of arriving at the correct location are remote. We will move from where we are, because all things change; we can only arrive where we want to go if we define or describe what the new locale will look like.

Quality targets can be simple or extremely complex, depending on the specific activity we are attempting to address. Here are some sample quality targets that might be used to describe scheduling:

SCHEDULING:

1. Fair
2. Efficient
3. Accessible
4. Communicated
5. Rational
6. Coordinated with Resources
7. Consistent

Each of the criteria, the sight, sound, smell, and texture of each descriptor can be elaborated as necessary in accordance with the size and complexity of the task at hand. For a small operation, the item "fair" might simply mean that each student or instructor has an equal allocation of available resources. "Efficient" might mean that minimal staff time is required to carry out scheduling functions. Minimal might be described as two hours per week.

A set of Quality Targets for the area of record keeping might look something like this:

RECORDS:

1. Complete
2. Accurate
3. Easy-Access
4. Secure
5. Up to Date
6. Consistent
7. Monitored
8. Legible
9. Consistent Process for Tracking

Having established Quality Targets for the various activities that make up a flight-training program, it would be appropriate to establish or adopt a data driven decision-making system to ensure continuous improvement. There are a number of models into which people have put considerable thought. One simple model is the Shewhart or PDAC Cycle: Plan, Do, Check, Act.

The Shewhart or PDAC Cycle is founded on the premise that quality lies in having clear, repeatable processes. Outcomes are seen as the inevitable result of process; if output is not as planned or as desired, it is the process that generates the outcome that must be modified. If we continue to do the same thing and are not happy with the results, we need to have a good look at what we are doing.

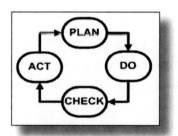

Diagram 1 Sheward or PDCA Cycle

The first phase of the PDAC cycle is to plan. During the "**Plan**" phase, processes are mapped out to ensure they are explored and understood and alternatives, as required, are developed. In addition, a means to measure outcome and effectiveness of the plan is initiated. Development of clear audit checklists can be extremely helpful at this stage.

In the second phase, "**Do**", the plan is implemented. Information derived from this phase is used to better inform and improve the Plan stage. It is critical during the "Do" phase that procedures are maintained in a consistent and stabilized manner. Unless consistent procedures are used, control over outcomes becomes impossible. The basic underlying understanding of producing positive change can be summed up as: if you want to change the outcome, you must first control the process.

The third phase, "**Check**", is focused on evaluation of how well the Plan is succeeding. If initial results or outcomes fall below expectations, modifications to the Plan can be implemented. Audit checklists are employed at this stage to provide a measure of success and to highlight areas of strength and weakness in the initial plan.

The final phase, "**Act**", is recognition of the effectiveness of the Plan. If required, the Plan will be modified to reflect information and measures obtained during the first three phases so that success is more likely.

The four phases form a repeating cycle of improvement toward the goal of achieving successful outcomes. If the Plan is not producing the desired outcomes, changes in the process are required.

To monitor and measure the effectiveness of our Plan, it is necessary to implement a Quality Audit system. Without a system of measuring outcomes, we are not able to systematically and positively effect change to our processes and are thereby unable to improve our outcomes.

The use of audit checklists focusing on specific areas of endeavour allows us to monitor and measure exactly what we are doing and provide us with empirical data upon which we can make decisions toward improvement. When we simply rely on feelings or anecdotal information to guide us, our decisions will always be haphazard, less than optimal. The increasingly difficult financial and social markets within which we operate are not tolerant of poor decision-making. Thirty percent of the FTUs offering training toward the CPL in Canada have gone out of business in the last 10 years.

The development of audit checklists is based on what are called "Quality Indicators", tools used to measure, monitor, and assess the quality of performance in a given area and to identify weaknesses in process that affect positive outcome. These Quality Indicators are generally broken down into three types: Structural Indicators, Process Indicators, and Outcome Indicators.

Structural Indicators describe characteristics of the *setting* that supports and has impact on the outcome of a process. They can be simple or complex. For example, the availability, organization, and accessibility of a required cleaning product might impact the ability to maintain aircraft in a clean condition. The failure of a heating system in the hangar could result in sub zero temperatures, resulting in grounding aircraft and loss of valuable training time.

> *Process Indicators* are used to *measure an activity* that is carried out toward the achievement of a quality target. They focus on the *amount and nature of activity* carried out toward a goal. For example, a quality target of 200 hours flight instruction per semester or 50 hours per month during a given time period, describes the expectation that an instructor maintain a measurable pace of flying that will allow the quality target to be achieved within a time frame. Failure to meet this quality target may impact the rate of student progress toward licence qualification.

> *Outcome Indicators* describe the *results of particular processes*. For example, one quality target for a FTU might be to provide excellent instruction. *Measures of the effectiveness* of the training could be reflected through scores on written and flight exams or the number of training hours above or below a national standard required to prepare a student for a particular licence or rating.

All three types of indicators—structural, process, and outcome—must be monitored and the results evaluated against desired outcomes.

A quality audit procedure is used to measure whether or not or to what degree quality indicators are being achieved. Quality audits are normally organized and implemented by the quality manager for each specific area of responsibility and are carried out on a scheduled basis. They are carried out using audit checklists based on appropriate quality indicators and prepared and developed by the quality manager in consultation with management. Where appropriate, quality audits in a FTU will include peer and or student assessment measures, as student and instructor satisfaction are critical factors in measuring and evaluating the success of an FTU.

A quality audit is designed to promote ongoing monitoring, best practice, open dialog, and continuous improvement within the various activities of the FTU program.

Following each audit, an audit report will be prepared by the quality manager and provided to the Chief Flight Instructor or Quality Assurance Manager and, perhaps, be presented to the instructor corps for review. The report will focus on documenting progress toward the achievement of quality targets and suggestions for improvement of policy, procedures, training, and measurement.

As an example, below is a sample Quality Audit Checklist developed to measure and monitor success with a university level program's student mentoring program. Each aviation student in this program is assigned to a senior instructor who monitors the student's progress, academic and flight training, within the aviation program and provides guidance and assistance, as required. The Quality Audit Checklist below was developed as a method to monitor and measure the effectiveness of the mentoring program.

Student Mentoring Program Audit Checklist (Sample)

ITEM	YES	NO
Mentoring is conducted in a quiet, private area.		
The instructor records pertinent information for each mentoring session.		
Mentoring session records are maintained and accessible		
Each student has a schedule for mentoring sessions.		
Records kept by the instructor show mentoring sessions have been conducted with each student at least once per month.		
Records kept by the instructor show each mentoring session has a duration of at least 15 minutes.		
The instructor provides each student with a questionnaire soliciting information regarding satisfaction levels, usefulness, and helpfulness of mentoring sessions.		
Student records indicate satisfactory progress in the Aviation Program or a plan for corrective action and instructor monitoring.		
Students report satisfaction with the mentoring process.		

Consistent quality is not the product of random actions and whimsical decision-making. It is the result, as William Foster wrote, of intelligent direction and skilful execution. Establishing a conscious system and methodology for identifying, describing, and responding in a planned way to observable and measurable outcomes allows normal people to consistently achieve high levels of quality.

Applying the basic principles of Quality Assurance to the flight-training environment allows the pursuit of quality flight training and significantly increases the likelihood of producing qualified and competent pilots to fill the coming needs of a growing industry.

NOTES:

Chapter 3.11

Strategic Thinking

"There were days when I was the safest pilot in the air. If that plane had crashed, I'd still be two miles behind it."
                    - Lt. Col. Doug Gillanders RCAF ret. (CF-104 Pilot)

Perhaps the greatest difference between experienced and inexperienced pilots is the experienced pilots' ability to think and process information with greater depth, the ability to focus more deeply on strategic rather than tactical thinking.

Tactical thinking and behaviours are characterized by a relatively narrow focus of attention, a reliance on skill-based response to stimuli, and minimal analysis and planning. Strategic thinking and behaviours are characterized by a relatively broader focus of attention and a deeper more knowledge-based processing of information involving evaluating, interpreting, assessing goals, and developing plans.

The ability to think and behave in a strategic manner, working with a broader event horizon, allows more connections to more information and context, expanding both forward and backward in time. More aspects of future situations and alternative scenarios can be considered.[14]

For individuals involved in tactical thinking and behaviour, acting takes precedence over thinking; for individuals involved primarily in strategic thinking, thinking, analyzing, and planning take precedence over acting.

Rasmussen[15] described a model of decision phases in the form of a decision ladder where shallow processing – skill-based behaviour – is shown as occurring at the bottom of the ladder and deeper processing – knowledge-based behaviour – is shown as extending from observations up the "analysis" leg and back down the "planning" leg to the response (see Fig 1).

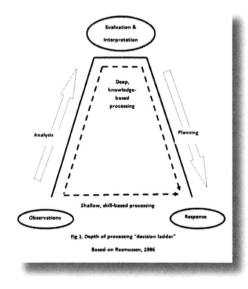

Fig 1. Depth of processing "decision ladder"
Based on Rasmussen, 1986

Some of the significant benefits in being able to operate from a strategic thinking and behaviour mode include a better-balanced workload, an enhanced ability to look into the future to analyze various scenarios, and an enhanced ability to take appropriate action earlier based on developing conditions. Strategic thinking provides an individual a considerable "performance advantage" as more information is available on which to base decisions, problem solving is enhanced, and better decisions are possible.

William Rogers points out, "There is a wealth of evidence that shows human performance is faster and more accurate when we know what to expect".[16] The ability to think and operate from a more strategic standpoint allows a pilot to work from a vantage point of significantly increased situational awareness: a bigger worldview.

As the Great One, Wayne Gretzky, said, "You want to be where the puck is going, not where it is."

Sadly, there does not seem to be a shortcut to experience. If it were "injectable", we would all, no doubt, be spared a considerable amount of confusion, embarrassment, pain, and aggravation. There is an old saying summing up the sad truth: "Experience is what you get right after you needed it."

Theory is a good step in helping us understand how things work so we can, hopefully, do what we need to do in the most efficient and effective manner possible. Practice and application is how we get it done.

As an instructor, a teacher, our job is not to despair the reality; any given person knows only what they know; students start where they are not where their instructor might hope they are. Our task is to create and maintain a positive learning environment within which a student is enabled to make the best and most positive progress of which he or she is capable.

How can we best enhance and encourage each student's ability to think and behave in a strategic manner while flying an aeroplane? Lewis Carroll wrote, "Begin at the beginning...and go on 'till you come to the end: then stop."

An old friend of mine, a teacher with more than 40 years experience, encouraged what he referred to as "peripatetic teaching", a teaching model based on the practice of Aristotle who taught philosophy while walking in the Lyceum of ancient Athens. The key here: use every moment. Each moment with a student is part of the teaching/learning process.

Start with the small things. We are looking for ways to minimize the amount of thinking process required to carry out tasks that can become part of muscle memory and make available as much of thinking capacity as possible for working with the bigger picture. If I am continually tripping over my shoe laces, it is hard to remember to look both ways before crossing the street, let alone consider where I am headed and for what purpose.

When working with students at the beginnings of their flying careers, make sure the most basic concepts and processes are well learned. Help students learn their way around a cockpit, for example. If more than two brain cells are required to find the throttle, mixture, carburetor heat, propeller, or flap controls, those additional brain cells are not available to be focused on a bigger picture.

Work on radio calls and procedures on the ground. Before starting in-flight instrument training, ensure the student is comfortable and relaxed with clearance shorthand. It's all the little distractions that bring us back to small mind and away from the bigger picture.

Encourage students to practice hangar-flying manoeuvres. Have them sit in the aeroplane on the ground, physically and verbally going through all the required motions, touching and moving all the appropriate controls in the correct sequence. When they are comfortable, have them do it eyes closed.

There is an excellent reason why the military requires recruits to disassemble and reassemble their weapons quickly and without visual reference. Familiarity allows a flow of process; it increases speed and it frees thinking capacity to analyze, plan, and consider.

In flight on the way to the practice area, asking questions about where we are, where we are going, what's going on, and what's likely to happen next all exercise the thought processes involved in projecting, analyzing, evaluating, and planning.

The process of answering questions helps students assemble and become conversant with the dialog that will, as they develop experience, allow that dialog to continue, grow, and mature.

The more basic skills and responses to situations can be "routinized", made routine and captured in the muscle memory, so they do not require significant thought activity while the more conscious mind can be devoted to thinking ahead: analyzing, evaluating, and planning. As Mr. Miyagi suggested, "Wax on; wax off."

Of course, in real-time operations, it is critical to balance analysis and planning with the need to perform immediate required tasks. Pure tactical behaviour increases reactivity at the expense of goal-directed behaviour; pure strategic behaviour can lead to inadequate flexibility in reacting to a changing environment.[17]

A pilot must find a satisfactory balance between strategic and tactical behaviour. We must always avoid the pothole in the road immediately in our path while, at the same time, remember and plan for our destination, Medicine Hat or Tickle Cove, many miles down that same road.

Experience is a product of time and time on task. It is something that is built, one piece at a time.

We can, however, enable its development by helping students make simple tasks routine through practice and repetition and by guiding the creation of the thought processes involved in working with the bigger picture. Ongoing practice, asking and answering the right questions, enhances the ability to ask those questions, and it opens the thought processes involved in projecting, analyzing, evaluating, and planning.

NOTES:

Chapter 3.12

Analysis of Flight Training Unit Performance

"Systems permit ordinary people to achieve extraordinary results, predictably. However, without a system, even extraordinary people find it difficult to predictably achieve even ordinary results."
-Michael Gerber

All institutions reflect the areas of strength and weakness of the people who operate them. Both the major strengths and weaknesses of most flight-training units emerge from the fact that they are operated by flight instructors

The obvious strength of flight instructors is that they, to one degree or another, know how to fly and have had some degree of training in how to provide instruction toward a pilot licence or rating.

If we are honest with ourselves, we must admit that many flight instructors are involved in flight training not because they love to teach and enjoy the process of working with students learning new and exciting skills. They are involved in flight training for a short period of time to earn the necessary flight hours required for them to move on to a "real" job in aviation: flying a bigger, faster aircraft.

Some small percentage of those involved in flight training is there because that is exactly what those people love to do: teach other people to fly. They derive deep satisfaction from the process of teaching and learning and are dedicated to providing the highest quality training possible for their students.

The result of the current and traditional structure of flight training in North America is that, for the most part, *ab initio* training is carried out by the least experienced and least trained personnel in the industry. The inevitable result of this structure is a noticeably high level of variance in the product: well-trained and skilled pilots.

Some instructors are excellent and tend to produce an excellent product. The majority of instructors, new to the industry and still finding their feet, through no direct fault of their own tend to produce a much more varied product: some good pilots, some just able to earn their licence. The variance in quality is high, and many flight-training units do not have the skills or knowledge to measure and control the level of quality they do produce.

Most major industries have been forced to move into the modern world of quality assurance to survive in the highly competitive business environment they must face. Witness the demise or near demise of some of our biggest corporate entities: Chrysler, General Motors, and Trans World Airlines. Failure to control the quality of product or service can have fatal consequences in a competitive environment.

Fortunately for us, in the world of flight training some very simple and inexpensive tools are now available to help us monitor and control the quality of our product: trained pilots.

In 1906, Vilfredo Pareto, an Italian economist working on a mathematical formula to describe wealth distribution in Italy, observed that 80% of the country's wealth was held by 20% of the population. I suspect very few of those in the top 20% were flight instructors.

In the late 1940's, Dr. Joseph Juran coined the phrase "Pareto's Principal" to describe the uneven, 20/80, distribution we have all experienced in various aspects of life: 20% of customers cause 80% of the problems; 20% of employees do 80% of the work, and so on.

There is no absolute in terms of 20/80 split; real life rarely maps itself to formulas. The key idea we can take away from this—an extremely useful idea to inform our decision-making—is that changing a few things can often result in significant benefits. The key is to identify those specific areas that cause the majority of our difficulties, or failures, or deviations from a standard or norm, so we can concentrate our efforts in the areas that cause or result in poor results most often.

One of the most basic tools of Quality Assurance—an approach to standardization of product used in most industries—is statistical analysis that allows us to monitor and correct variance in our product on an ongoing basis.[18] The key concept is to employ tools that allow us to see what we are actually doing and to take corrective actions, as required, to improve both the quality and consistency of our product output.

If we want to fix a problem we need to know what it is. We need a way to "see" it.

One area where this technique can be applied is in analysis of performance: the outcomes of our training program. In flight training, one of the concrete measurement tools we can use to measure outcomes of our training program are the results achieved by our students on flight test. Every one of our students earning a multi-engine rating or a recreational pilot licence must pass an identical flight test conducted by trained and certified examiners who mark against objective standards.

While certainly not the only measurement of quality, the flight test does give us hard measured data to use as an evaluative baseline. In Canada, one outcome for an instructor with 3 or more flight test failures out of the last 10 recommendations is a visit from his or her friendly Transport Canada inspector for a chat.

One exam, of course, tells us about a particular student on a particular day. A larger number of exams begin to tell us about our training program. We can start to see, to uncover, the patterns.

In terms of applying corrective action, we need to see the trends and patterns. Relying on anecdotal evidence: "All seems to be going OK except for Rachael and Bob," is not nearly as powerful a diagnostic tool as finding that over the past six months 12% of our students have earned low flight test marks on Short Field Landings or ADF Holds.

The Pareto Diagram, see diagram 1, represents low exam scores, failing or marginal scores, on the Multi-Engine Instrument Rating flight test over a three year period at a university level flight training unit.[19] In Canada, flight test are scored on a 4 point scale: a score of 4 indicates above standard performance; 3 indicates performance within the standard; 2 indicates deviations from the standard that are corrected in a timely fashion, and 1 represents unacceptable deviations from the standard or unsafe flying. Candidates for a licence or rating must achieve a sufficient number of total points and no scores of 1 to earn a pass mark on the flight test.

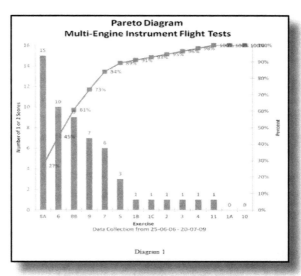

Diagram 1, The Pareto Diagram

For the purposes of this analysis, flight test results from the chosen time period were evaluated and the number of 1 or 2 scores for each exercise on the flight tests was recorded. Looking at Diagram 1, we can see that 15 Instrument Rating candidates earned a score 1 or 2 on exercise 8A, NDB Approaches and only 1 candidate earned a score of 1 or 2 on exercise 11, Emergency Procedures, for example.

There are a sufficient number of exams to show useful results in terms of decision-making. The Pareto Diagram orders items in terms of "most first", allowing a visual separation of the "vital few" from the "trivial many". In this case, the data are recorded as number of low scores (scores of 1 or 2 out of a 4 point scale). The Pareto Diagram allows us to identify and highlight which specific exercises are the most problematic for the largest number of students so corrective action can be taken.

In its wisdom, the FAA, as I understand it, uses a binary marking format: pass/fail. While this may mask some of the gradations in evaluating licence candidate performance, it can still be used to investigate areas of weak performance based on the number of students who fail to achieve a pass mark on specific exercises.

On any given day, any given student can achieve a low score on a particular flight test exercise. What we are particularly interested in here is overall patterns. What we are hoping to do is identify areas of weakness in our training program.

Unless we can see the problem areas, we cannot apply corrective measures.

Looking at the diagram and following the nice red line which indicates the total percentage of results cumulatively, we can see that one item, exercise 8A, NDB Approaches, accounts for almost one third, 27% of all the low scores achieved by students over the given time period. Five of the 16 exercises that make up the exam, 31%, account for 84% of all low scores.

Pending a more detailed investigation, taking a good look at how those five exercises are being taught and how student performance is being evaluated prior to flight test recommendation doesn't seem like a bad plan. We want to put our energy and focus for improvement where it will make the most difference.

Of course, as William Watt said, "Do not put your faith in what statistics say until you have carefully considered what they do not say."

It may also be very useful to compare scores for students of individual instructors, assuming an instructor has recommended a sufficient number of students to demonstrate a pattern. If all of our instructors save one or two are achieving acceptable results, rather than adjust our training program it may be more useful to provide additional training for the individual instructor(s).

As a training institution, we need to know what we are doing well and what we are doing poorly. We need to be able to put focus on areas of weakness and take corrective action in a timely fashion. We do not need to accept poor or irregular performance.

Making use of some simple statistical analysis tools allows us to review how we are conducting our training and evaluation and make positive decisions on appropriate changes to our training programs. We can have the tools to "see" what is actually going on: where are we strong and where are we performing below the standard we are willing to accept, so we can make informed decisions about our methods and procedures to ensure a stable and positive set of quality outcomes: well trained, skilled pilots.

NOTES:

Chapter 3.13

Cultural Differences

"It is not part of a true culture to tame tigers, any more than it is to make sheep ferocious."

-Henry David Thoreau

It's been a fairly busy time, the last month or so. Summer students have been completing their programs either in preparation for entry into the university program this fall or in an effort to avoid the unavoidable delays resulting from the coming fall and winter weather. The end of the good flying season is always an interesting time.

In reviewing my flight test reports I am reminded what a diverse cultural environment we enjoy out here on the "left" coast of Canada. Just going by surnames, I have conducted flight tests over the past month with candidates whose family heritages are British, French, Polish, Russian, Austrian, Italian, Swiss, German, Indian, Japanese, Vietnamese, Dutch, Indonesian, Filipino, and Chinese. Almost all of them have been successful on their first try, which makes them, their instructors, and their flight examiner quite happy.

It is an interesting adventure, working with people from a variety of different cultural backgrounds toward the common goal of becoming pilots. To be an effective and efficient instructor, or flight test examiner, does call for some appreciation of the differences, the strengths, the positive aspects of various cultures, and their approaches to learning in this complex environment we call aviation.

If we think of our genetic coding as our essential "hardware", culture can be understood as our "software".

Culture, itself, is an interesting concept. To paraphrase Edward B. Taylor, English anthropologist, who was the first to use the term culture, it "...is the full range of learned human behaviour patterns."[20] It is, one might say, the social water in which we swim. There is an old saying that no one knows who discovered water, but we know for certain it wasn't a fish. We only "notice" our culture when we come in contact with those who do not share it.

Cultural values learned initially from our parents and immediate family and later from our wider social interactions tend to define how we answer questions about good and bad, dangerous and safe, dirty and clean, ugly and beautiful, abnormal and normal. The answers to these questions are not always universal; different cultures tend to have different answers. The more insular our upbringing, the more difficulty we tend to have as adults accepting that others may not share our particular set of values.

We may find it very difficult to change who we are and what we believe to be true; most people do, but we can come to appreciate and learn that others are who they are and bring with them to the learning environment their own web of cultural values and behaviours. As instructors, we can incorporate this appreciation into our ways of interacting and helping those who come to us to learn.

Greert Hofstede, a Dutch researcher in the fields of organizational studies and organizational culture, wrote that different cultures inculcate different solutions to the same five basic problems.[21] These problems or questions are about how we deal with:

- Inequality,
- The need for security,
- Relationships with others,
- Emotional gender roles, and
- Time horizons.

The question of inequality focuses on power distance between individuals, whether it is large or small. The question of security revolves around our level of uncertainty avoidance, how well we can be comfortable with "not knowing". Relationships with others include our focus on individualism or collectivism. Emotional gender roles relate to our concepts of masculinity and femininity.

Our cultural sense of time horizon gives us guidance toward either short term or long-term solutions. In cultures with a more long term orientation, members of the society are encouraged to adapt themselves and work toward a desirable future; in cultures with a more short term orientation, members are encouraged to take guidance from the past and try to fulfill their present needs and desires in relation to that past.

Keeping in mind there is considerable variation within any given culture, Hofstede gives us some general guidance that can be very helpful in understanding how best to work with students from various cultural backgrounds. As George Clooney's character in *Up in the Air* says, "I stereotype; it's faster."

For the sake of brevity, let's tackle the first two cultural problems: inequality and the need for security. For a broader yet quick overview of Hofstede's work, have a look at the PDF document listed in the endnotes.[22]

Students from the Nordic and Anglo countries, the USA, the Netherlands, German speakers, the Baltic States, Hungary, and Israel all tend to have a relatively low sense of power distance. Students from China, India, Latin countries, Czechia, Poland, Korea, Japan and Russia tend to have a much stronger sense of power distance.

Students from cultures that encourage a large power distance tend to be more comfortable with a dependency on teachers, treat teachers with a high level of respect, favour a teacher centered learning model, and tend to see teachers as those who transfer personal wisdom to their students.

Students from cultures that encourage a small power distance tend to treat teachers as equals, favour a student-centred learning model, are much more able to initiate communications in a learning environment, and tend to see teachers as experts who transfer impersonal truths.

Neither approach is inherently good or bad, positive or negative. Appreciating our students' different cultural values can help us, as instructors, be more efficient and effective. It's pretty much a case of not fighting with that which we can't and don't really need to change in order to achieve our particular goal: helping people learn the skills and knowledge necessary to be safe and competent aviators.

Students from the Nordic and Anglo countries, the Netherlands, the USA, China, and India tend to have a weak sense of uncertainty avoidance, a fairly well established ability to live with uncertainty. Students from German speaking countries, the Baltic States, Hungary, Israel, Latin countries, Czechia, Poland, Korea, Japan, and Russia tend to have a stronger sense of uncertainty avoidance.

Students with strong uncertainty avoidance tend to prefer their instructors to provide the right answers and to have all the answers. There may be a strong pressure among these students to conform. Students with a weaker sense of uncertainty avoidance prefer good discussions. They are comfortable with an instructor using the words, "That's a good question, but I don't know the answer right now." They are relatively tolerant of differences among students in a class.

As part of initial instructor training, instructor candidates are generally exposed to a brief introduction on various learning models and cultural differences. We may have heard some ideas about kinetic, auditory and visual learning; we may have heard some words about cultural differences. To be a really effective and efficient instructor, however, developing a deeper sense of understanding of cultural differences and learning how to adapt our approach to allow students to learn in the most efficient manner for them can be both helpful and very satisfying.

As a flight instructor, it is not part of my function to change my students' beliefs or cultural values. It is my function to provide them with a positive and efficient learning environment and to help them become safe and proficient pilots.

NOTES:

Chapter 3.14

Using YouTube Videos as Teaching Aids

"Good teaching is one-forth preparation and three-fourths theatre."
-Gail Goodwin

Individuals and a number of well funded institutions with experienced professional staff have entered into the field of producing aviation related and focused training videos for various aspects of aviation and have made these resources available at no cost via YouTube. Instructors are beginning to incorporate and use these materials in their ground school and flight training programs with excellent results.

Many of the videos available for free via YouTube are one-off adventures highlighting particular events or moments; some are well researched, well orchestrated materials specific to training. Both of these types of materials can be very useful to pilots, pilots-in-training, and instructors.

Many pilots continue to be interested in improving their skills and knowledge but may not be able or willing to target personal funding to avail themselves of additional training materials that can represent considerable investment. Many smaller flight-training units do not have the resources, personnel, or funding to produce training materials of the quality and depth now available for free on the Internet. The production and availability of these materials can be of tremendous benefit to the aviation training community by making high quality training materials available to anyone with a basic computer and access to the Internet.

In aviation, it is extremely difficult to know too much. Talking advantage of the wisdom and experience of others is an excellent plan, regardless of where on the learning continuum we may find ourselves.

One excellent example of a one-off production is a video filmed by the passengers of a beautifully restored Stinson 108 attempting a high density altitude takeoff resulting in a crash. It is a unique, first-hand account of an accident filmed from the cockpit. No doubt the intention of the videographers was not to film the sequence of events leading up to and progressing through the accident and its aftermath, but that is what was achieved.

The video provides an outstanding learning/teaching aid for exploring the challenges of high density altitude operations and the inherent risks involved. It is also an excellent, "set-the-stage" teaching aid to kick off a discussion and exploration of the pilot decision making process, the importance of incorporating SOPs into our practice, and flying techniques required to mitigate risk in potentially difficult situations. In this particular case, for example, failure to properly lean the engine to achieve full power on takeoff was, most likely, a contributing factor to the end result, as was the failure to establish a go/no go point prior to initiating the takeoff roll. [23]

I have made use of this little video in both private and commercial ground schools with excellent results. The video provides a rare, "you are there", view of the events: the difficulties experienced by the pilot on takeoff, the failure to achieve altitude, and the subsequent crash in rising terrain.

Prior to showing the film, I will normally have covered the basic groundwork of defining and calculating density altitude, exploring the takeoff and performance charts and tables provided in the aircraft POH, and working through various example problems involving aircraft performance from various airports and aerodromes for which information is available to the students. A discussion regarding pilot decision making, SOPs, and the importance of appreciating the concept of accelerate stop distance and risk mitigation will also be included in the lead up to viewing the film.

Once students have a basic understanding of density altitude and its effects on aircraft performance, pilot decision making models, and risk mitigation based on a reasonable understanding of aircraft performance in various conditions, I will show the film as a good starter for discussion and exploration.

I find giving students an opportunity to see, as though they were sitting in the cockpit of the aeroplane, the full sequence of the accident provides an excellent motivation to, "dig in" and analyze the various factors leading to the accident and to focus on how such events can be prevented.

On a broader scale, there are a number of excellent video series productions, available on YouTube, created specifically for flight training. As examples, I have found the materials produced by the University of North Dakota aviation program and the series produced by Mr. Ray Preston, former Chief Flight Instructor at Selkirk College, very useful.

The University of North Dakota is one of the leading university aviation programs in North America. They have created a series of training videos that are well organized, well presented, and very useful both for training and for increasing pilot knowledge. While some of the references in this series of excellent videos are specific to the UND training program and UND SOPs, I highly recommend an exploration of these materials to pilots, pilots-in-training, and instructors. I use a variety of these materials both in ground school and for flight training and believe they have been extremely helpful both for pilots-in-training and for me as an instructor. The topics covered in this series extend from *ab initio* through advanced training. [24]

For instructors interested in anything from executing normal landings, dealing with wake turbulence, or successfully completing ILS approaches these videos can be an excellent resource.

Mr. Ray Preston, former Chief Flight Instructor at Selkirk College, has produced a series of videos designed specifically to help teach initial instrument rating candidates the theory and procedures of using GPS to execute that difficult manoeuvre, the hold. The videos take a detailed and in-depth look at using GPS to facilitate hold entry and maintenance of a successful hold, including compensating for various wind conditions. For both students in the process of learning instrument procedures and instructors involved in teaching these sometimes-complex procedures, this series of videos is an outstanding resource. [25]

These examples do not in any way represent the totality of the resources available; I encourage pilots, pilots-in-training, and instructors to investigate the wide variety of available materials that may be useful and helpful to their specific purposes.

The availability of valuable and free materials that can be used to enhance and personalize a learning environment and program with very positive results is growing. While the materials themselves do not provide a full learning environment, incorporating them as part of a lesson can assist an instructor to provide students with an experiential and personalized component. It may not quite be quite as effective as actually having an experience, but it may allow us, as instructors, to come much closer to achieving in a classroom environment a very positive and productive learning environment.

NOTES:

Chapter 3.15

Flight Training Programs

"There is nothing wrong with change, if it is in the right direction."
-Winston Churchill

When I was in university an older acquaintance of mine, a serving infantry officer in the US Army, was promoted and sent to advanced officer training prior to being deployed to Viet Nam for his second tour. Being a curious type, I asked him what exactly they taught him during his training. His reply: Korea.

As humans, we all seem to share a fixation on applying previous experience to new situations. We might think of ourselves as a collection of solutions waiting for a problem. Unfortunately, all too often we continue to apply solutions that worked on previous problems long after they have proven inadequate. As Marshall McLuhan wrote, "We look at the present through a rear-view mirror. We march backwards into the future." I'm sure we can all think of specific examples.

To our credit, our current flight training system is excellent and is the product of years and years of close study and reflection. It is grounded on a sound and well-studied body of experience; it has served us well. Projecting it into the future, however, may be something we will have to examine carefully. As a friend of mine said to me the other day, "We have an excellent program for training bush pilots."

The training model we have inherited and have been using successfully for years and is based on a linear developmental model: we start at Alpha and work steadily and sequentially toward Zulu: PPL, CPL, Multi, IFR. First, we train pilots to fly light single engine aircraft in VFR conditions. Then, to paraphrase Yogi Berra, we come to a fork in the road and take it.

We train budding pilots to fly aircraft with more than one engine or one on floats. Following close behind, we train them to fly aircraft with reference to instruments in preparation for flight in IMC, perhaps as a second pilot. During their apprentice period flying as second pilot, they will hopefully have an opportunity to receive further training and experience to qualify them to sit in the left seat of complex, modern aircraft.

We expect and anticipate a new pilot to follow some variation on the traditional career path: either instructor or bush pilot, charter pilot, regional or small carrier pilot, and then, at long last, airline pilot: a linear progression through the ranks of aviation. Of course, many if not most pilots will drop out along the way for the variety of reasons we all know: money, time, boredom, lack of commitment, fear, or, perhaps, failure to develop the required skills. It is a linear, sequential, analog model that has worked and made sense to us for several generations.

Sadly or fortunately — an assessment dependant on our age and temperament — our world has moved decidedly from a linear, sequential, analog reality to a non-linear, non-sequential, digital reality. What comes next no longer necessarily connects with what came before.

Our world of aviation, too, is experiencing an accelerating rate of change. The technology of flight has advanced in an exponential curve rather than a linear manner and, if we are not to find ourselves far, far behind the curve, some investigation and consideration of what exactly we are training people for and what that training should encompass will have to be undertaken.

It is now possible to fly a large aircraft from Vancouver to Singapore while sipping coffee sitting in your office in Toronto or Winnipeg, or Regina or, heaven forbid, Topeka, Kansas. Targets the size of a moving pickup truck in Iran or Afghanistan are being destroyed by unmanned aircraft flown by operators sitting in the comfort of an office in Kansas, or is it Florida?

Most air travelers are probably not quite ready for the "pilotless" aircraft, but that is a psychological and social barrier rather than a technological one. The technology is there, and it is being used; the most significant performance barriers in military fighter aircraft are the limitations imposed by the physiology of pilots not the limitations of the technology.

The actual "job" of modern airline pilots is moving rapidly from controlling heavy machines toward monitoring the complex computer systems that control the big machines.

Even smaller GA aircraft are moving in the same direction. I had an opportunity to fly with a friend in his new Columbia the other day; it reminded me more of a TV studio than what I am used to as an aircraft. There were flashing screens, virtual dials, and a soft female voice reporting traffic and proximity alerts all during the flight. Once the machine is airborne, as long as you've told it where to go, it will simply take you there by the route you have pre-selected. If we'd had the nerves to do it, I'm sure we could have set an alarm to wake us up just prior to or at decision altitude, necessary only because the machine was not equipped with auto-land.

For good reasons, aviation is a very conservative endeavour. Very few people are willing to fly the "A" model of anything or change a routine, procedure, or pattern that has proven successful, and our system of training pilots follows that same conservative pattern. It may be, however, that that pattern will no longer serve us well into the future.

When I was in high school, we spent hours learning how to use a slide rule or log tables to calculate problems in chemistry and physics. Students can now solve much more complex problems in a small fraction of the time with the use of software and computers and never actually have to understand the underlying process involved. They plug the right inputs into the right machine in the approved manner and arrive at the correct solution.

In university I was taught to use a ruling pen, a 15th century graphic tool that would have been a familiar piece of equipment to Christopher Columbus, to make maps. Contemporary cartographers use satellite and aerial imaging and computers to create maps accurate to within millimeters.

We older folk can put all the moral spin we choose to this change; yet, there it is. And it appears to be working with great success.

It may well be time to begin phasing out the program of the past, at least for advanced piloting programs, and begin substituting in the real skills that are involved in conducting the process of flight in modern machines, at least for those destined or selected to conduct such machines. More and more training institutions are taking a closer look at the new, ICAO multi-crew licensing requirements, allowing pilots to achieve certification to fly in a multi crew environment only.

It may be that the interim period, the next decade or so, will have to face the reality of a two-tiered flight training system: one for those who will continue to fly the out-dated, toy flying machines we have inherited from the past, and one for those who will enter the world of aviation in the future. I will leave the details to those who will move into that future, but I can certainly see it on the near horizon.

NOTES:

(Endnotes)

1 Reyno, Mike, "Finding the School Right for You," Wings Aviation Magazine, issue #1, Vol. 42, March/April 2001. pp10-11

2 http://caac.ca

3 http://www.tc.gc.ca/eng/civilaviation/regserv/cars/part4-401-1073.htm#401_05

4 Gladwell, Malcolm, Outliers: The Story of Success, Little, Brown and Company, November 18, 2008

5 http://www.tc.gc.ca/Publications/en/tp975/pdf/hr/tp975e.pdf

6 http://selair.selkirk.ca/Flight_Planning/C-172-chart.html

7 http://www.wingsmagazine.com/content/view/1122/38/

8 http://www.tsb.gc.ca/eng/rapports-reports/aviation/2008/a08p0353/a08p0353.asp

9 http://www.sciencedaily.com/

10 Lipshitz, R. (1993), Converging Themes in the study of Decision-making in Realistic Settings. In Decision-making in Action: Models and Methods, G.S. Klien, J. Orasanu, R. Calderwood, and C. E. Asambok (eds), pp 105-109, 1993.

11 http://www.ntsb.gov/safety/mwl-2.html2

12 http://www.tsb.gc.ca/eng/stats/aviation/2010/ss10.asp

13 http://www.atac.ca/web/images/atac/files/HR_Report_on_the_Commercial_Pilot_in_Canada-Final_version.pdf

14 Rogers, William H. Thinking Ahead: Using Strategic Behavior to Avoid Errors on the Commercial Flight Deck" presented at Human Error, safety and Systems Development symposium, 1998, http://www.des.gla.ac.uk/~johnson/papers/seattle_hessd/WR_strat-p.pdf

15 Rasmussen, J. (1986). Information processing and human-machine interaction: An approach to cognitive engineering. New York: Elsevier Science Publishers.

16 Rogers, William H. Thinking Ahead: Using Strategic Behavior to Avoid Errors on the Commercial Flight Deck" presented at Human Error, safety and Systems Development symposium, 1998, http://www.des.gla.ac.uk/~johnson/papers/seattle_hessd/WR_strat-p.pdf

17 Bonissone, P.P., Dutta, S., & Wood, N.C. (1994). Merging strategic and tactical planning in dynamic and uncertain environments. IEEE Transactions on Systems, Man, and Cybernetics, 24, 841-862.

18 One very helpful resource is the book, "The Memory Jogger, A Pocket Guide of Tools for Continuous Improvement & Effective Planning," by Michael Brassard & Diane Ritter. Website: www.goalqpc. com.

19 In Canada, Instrument Ratings are grouped by the type or types of aircraft the pilot is licenced to fly under IFR conditions. A Group 1 Instrument Rating is issued to successful candidates who complete at least 5 hours of their IFR training in a side-by-side multi-engine aircraft and successfully pass their IR flight test in a side-by-side ME aircraft. The holder of a Group 1 Instrument Rating may fly side-by-side ME aircraft, inline ME aircraft and single engine aircraft IFR.

20 Tylor, Edward. 1920 [1871]. Primitive Culture. New York: J.P. Putnam's Sons

21 Hofstede, Greert, Culture's Consequences, Safe Publications, 2455 Teller Road, Thousand Oaks, California, 2001

22 http://fuhu.dk/filer/FBE/Arrangementer/Denmark%20 Unlimited%20080508/FBE_geert_hofstede_teaching_learning.pdf

23 http://www.youtube.com/watch?v=yDu0jYiz-v8

24 http://www.youtube.com/user/undaerocast?feature=watch

25 http://www.youtube.com/watch?v=4H7QcWCDIzQ

PART 4 HUMAN FACTORS

Chapter 4.1

Visual Focal Points

"Fix your eyes on perfection and you make almost everything speed towards it."

-William Ellery Channing

When we make a mistake or do something that does not meet our satisfaction we frequently ask the question, "What was I thinking?" This is a reasonable response and may possibly lead us to some valuable insights. I often find, however, when working with students learning to fly a more vital question is, "Where was I looking?"

Where we look, where we focus our visual attention when flying is in many ways a more positive indicator of how we will perform than what we are thinking.

What we think directs where our mind goes; where we look is where the aircraft goes.

Taxiing, turns, and slips are all excellent examples of manoeuvres illustrating the relationship between visual focus and performance. A moment's thought will suggest many more.

When taxiing an aircraft, we must learn to coordinate feet, hands, and eyes to keep the machine tracking and manoeuvring as required. Particularly during the early stages of training, it is critical to form a connection between eyes and feet if we are to keep the machine anywhere near the centerline of the taxiway. We need to find a focal point for our eyes to achieve the required taxi pathway.

Many people have little or no experience controlling things with their feet, so the initial learning process can be comical at times. I know mine was. The big exception, as most flight instructors will tell you, is those people who have operated tracked vehicles: they have developed excellent eye-foot coordination. Soccer players, as well, tend to find use of rudder pedals coordinated with eye focus much easier than the average person.

Just as with driving a car, if we set our focal point too close to the front of the aircraft we find ourselves overcorrecting, swerving right and left down the taxiway. I like to tell students to look down the taxiway line, if there is one, and find the point ahead along the line where motion ceases.

Too close a focal point and the line appears to be moving. We need to find the "still" point and keep our eyes focused there.

When learning turns, where we focus our eyes is very important if we want to achieve success. Many young pilots and students pilots have spent hours and hours in front of their computer playing with a flight simulator. Instruments are very familiar to them and very comforting.

When flying VFR, however, we do not want to have our eyes focused inside the cockpit on the instrument panel. We do want to be in direct visual contact with the earth's surface, the horizon and the airspace surrounding our aircraft.

Once again, where our eyes go is where the aircraft goes. If we are flying from the left seat and looking down at the instruments while performing a turn to the left, for example, typically the aircraft will dive to the left as it turns; as we turn to the right, typically, the aircraft will climb as it turns. Our eyes are not providing our muscles with appropriate information.

To enter a turn, conduct a good lookout to be sure you are safe to manoeuvre, focus your eyes on the horizon about 30° ahead of the nose in the direction of the turn, and guide the aircraft through the turn. It's a very similar act to shooting a moving target: you must project where the target will be and lead the target with your eyes. The aircraft will naturally follow where you look once the connections have been established between your eyes and your muscles.

Many instructors will help students focus outside during turns by reaching over and covering the instruments. It's quite amazing to see how much better a student will perform once he or she gets over the burst of irritation resulting from the "taking away" their normal input source.

Slips are a particularly useful manoeuvre, but can be very disorienting, particularly in the early stages of training. Even many experienced pilots hesitate to slip an aircraft if they can find another solution. Done correctly, however, slipping is a very useful, elegant, and elegant manoeuvre.

Set yourself up to enter a slip by establishing the aircraft in a power-off glide at best glide speed. Note the aircraft's attitude in relation to the horizon and pick a stationary object or point on the ground ahead along your flight path. Preferably, pick something at about the point you would touch down if the glide continued, or slightly beyond.

Roll the aircraft into a bank; stop the turn with rudder. Keep your eyes on the focal point during the entire manoeuvre and allow the aircraft to fly toward it. Or rather, allow yourself to fly toward it and bring the aircraft with you. Keep full opposite rudder application so you only have one set of control inputs to deal with. You can easily judge whether to add or reduce aileron input and whether or not your pitch attitude must be adjusted because you have a fixed point of reference. To recover, reduce rudder and aileron inputs gently and simultaneously to neutral while keeping your eyes on the same focal point.

Disorientation is eliminated, and, if anyone happens to be watching, they will surely say, "What a pretty job that fellow did."

If we want to execute a slipping turn, we simply apply the same technique we used in a level turn: project our path, lead with our focal point and guide the aircraft with our eyes.

Paying attention to where we look when we fly, particularly when we manoeuvre the machine, can be invaluable in improving our performance. If you're not certain where you have been looking, remind yourself to notice. We can all find ways to improve our piloting skills.

Enjoy.

NOTES:

Chapter 4.2

Rain

"I'm never gonna stop the rain by complaining..."

-BJ Thomas

If there's one thing we have in good measure out here in lower BC, it's rain. I can't speak for the rest of the country, but I suspect rain is to be found in other jurisdictions as well.

Even as I write these words, I glance outside and what do I see? Good guess: rain falling gently to the ground, soaking into the grass verges, pooling on the runway and taxiways.

Aircraft operations are affected by rain in a number of ways, and it is a very good plan to understand the challenges presented. Visibility is reduced and distorted. Take off and landing rolls are increased. Control problems may occur. Opportunities for the formation of carburetor ice with carbureted engines are greatly increased.

One option, of course, is to leave the aircraft tied down whenever any sign of rain threatens. This may well be a good option for many recreational and low time pilots. It is important to know your personal limits and to stick by them.

Another option is to develop the necessary base of knowledge, skills, and experience to reduce the risks of operating in the potentially difficult conditions rain produces.

Rain affects a pilot's vision in three major ways, all of them negatively. The most obvious is that rain limits both the quantity of light available to the pilot's eyes and the forward distance a pilot can see. Rain is almost always associated with cloud layers that reduce the overall amount of ambient light available.

Before commencing any flight, confirm that the required minimum visibility conditions exist and are forecast to exist for an appropriate time period. Temperature and dew point spreads can be very important information for flight planning in marginal conditions. A temperature/dew-point spread that has been decreasing over the last few hours — METARs are a good source of information — indicate things are not going in a positive direction: when the temperature and dew-point differential drops to within 2^0C, we can expect fog will develop and visibility may become a thing of the past.

Rain on the windscreen of our aircraft also produces some very interesting effects resulting from a combination of refraction, a bending of light, and diffusion, a spreading out of the ambient light.

All of us have, at one time or another, stuck our hand or a stick into water and seen the hand or stick "bend". This phenomenon is called refraction. Light passing through the medium of water changes direction giving an illusion the object we are looking at is displaced from its actual position.

Refraction of light through the medium of water can result in our seeing objects outside at a different altitude than they would normally appear. Tops of hills, other obstacles, and the horizon itself will appear lower than they actually are. The general rule of thumb is that objects half a mile ahead of our aircraft may appear to be as much as 200 feet lower than actual, roughly a 4.5° refraction ($\tan \theta = 200/2640$).

If you want to really appreciate this illusion, drop a penny in a sink full of water and try to pick it up with one grab, first try.

This phenomenon is important to understand both for terrain clearance and during landings and takeoffs. I always try to take student pilots flying in the rain at some point during their training, so they can experience firsthand the illusions resulting from rain on the windscreen. It's one thing to talk about things in a theoretical way; it's another entirely to experience firsthand at 100 Knots.

Light passing through water as well as being refracted is diffused, spread apart. The result is two interesting effects: lighted objects in the distance will appear less bright and farther away, and lighted objects close up will appear larger than they actually are. Diffusion of light energy reduces the apparent intensity of the source and spreads the radiated light over a greater area.

Lighted objects, such as runway lights seen at close range, because of the diffusion of their light, will appear larger than they actually are; our poor little brains will be tempted to interpret this information to mean that the lights are closer than they actually are.

Takeoff and landing distances are affected by standing water on the runway. We are all familiar with the takeoff and landing performance charts or graphs or tables for the aircraft we normally fly. Landing on a dry grass runway, for example, can increase our landing roll by 45% or more.

Landing on a wet grass runway could easily double or triple our required landing distance. As we all remember from our younger days, wet grass closely resembles ice in terms of its "slipperiness."

While specific numbers are probably not provided in your POH for calculating landing distances on wet runways, the Canadian Runway Friction Index (CRFI) gives us valuable, performance information.

The CRFI is a measurement system used to indicate how slippery a runway is as a result of water, snow, or ice. A clear example with explanation of a CRFI chart is provided in section A of your Canadian Flight Supplement.

A CRFI reading of 1.0 indicates maximal effective braking; readings between 1.0 and 0.8 indicate the best possible braking conditions: a bare, dry runway. Equivalent braking action would be described as Good.

Damp conditions with 0.01" to 0.03" of water on the runway surface would give us a CFRI of 0.6 to 0.3. Equivalent braking action would be described as Fair to Poor: an increase in landing roll of between 45%-99% can be anticipated.

Heavy rain with 0.03" to 0.1" of standing water will result in a CRFI reading of 0.3 to 0.0: an increase in landing roll of 100% or more can be anticipated. Equivalent braking action would be described as Poor to Nil.

The CRFI also provides a good indication of the maximum crosswind tolerance in the ambient conditions.

Control problems can result from the presence of water on the takeoff and landing surface through the process known as hydroplaning. There are three types of hydroplaning, and it is useful to be familiar with all three.

Dynamic hydroplaning may occur when there is standing water on the runway surface. The standing water exerts a pressure between the aircraft tires and the runway surface causing the tires to lift. The tires lose their contact with the surface.

When dynamic hydroplaning occurs, steering is not effective; braking may be ineffective and may, indeed, lead to worse difficulties. Strong crosswinds may simply push an aircraft off the runway. Until the aircraft has slowed below the hydroplaning speed, we may resemble a pig on ice more than we might ideally choose.

Even though we are in contact with the ground, our control of the aircraft will be produced by use of our flying surfaces: aileron, elevator, and rudder rather than the landing gear steering system.

A rule of thumb for predicting dynamic hydroplaning speed in knots is given by the formula 8.6 x √tire pressure, psi. A tire pressure of 25 psi will result in a minimum dynamic hydroplaning speed of 43 knots.[1] At any speed above 43 knots, we can expect to experience dynamic hydroplaning, both on landing and takeoff, given the right conditions.

Viscous hydroplaning can occur on areas of the runway where it has been painted or where there are rubber deposits from landing aircraft. Paint or rubber deposits make the runway slick, and moisture creates a film over the slick surface resulting in loss of tire traction. Skidding may occur, resulting in loss of control. Viscous hydroplaning may occur at a much lower speed than dynamic hydroplaning and can cause control problems even while taxiing.

Reverted rubber hydroplaning is a condition that is created through improper use of brakes. If we apply brakes at touchdown on a wet runway, the aircraft will enter dynamic hydroplaning: the wheels will lock. As the aircraft slides down the runway, water between the tires and the runway surface will heat up and a layer of steam and molten rubber will develop between the tire and the surface.

We are now riding down the runway on a layer of very slippery material that we create as we go. A serious danger of reverted rubber hydroplaning is that the condition can continue down to virtually zero speed and seriously affect our ability to control the aircraft.

Carburetor icing in rainy conditions can be a safety factor if you fly an aircraft with a carbureted fuel system. I think we might leave an in depth coverage of this topic for another time, but suffice it to say, carburetor icing is something to be very, very alert for when flying in damp and rainy conditions. Learn the symptoms and the appropriate procedures for your particular aircraft. Know them well.

Since we do get our share—some would say more than our fair share— of rain, it's a good plan to either learn to deal with it effectively or to stay on the ground when it is or threatens to be rainy. The decision to remain on the ground in rainy conditions can be a very good one, particularly if you have not developed the necessary base of knowledge, skills and experience.

If you do choose or must fly during periods of rain, tackle the problem: learn the illusions, performance limitations and challenges, and find a safe way to explore the reality first hand so you can gain the necessary experience.

NOTES:

Chapter 4.3

Winter Vision

"The machine does not isolate man from the great problems of nature but plunges him more deeply into them."
                                                                    -Antoine de Saint-Exupery

An old friend of mine used to tell a joke the body of which I have forgotten. The punch line, however, was something to the effect that, "If you need to store something in a cool dark place try Canada"

Now, we mustn't be too negative; there are several months during which it would be uncharitable to describe Canada as a cool dark place. The winter months, however, even in the banana belt of Southern BC, can certainly include times when ambient light levels could be accurately described as low and visual challenges become an important part of our flying lives.

We have all heard again and again about the challenges involved with cold, ice or snow-covered runways, icing conditions, survival precautions, and the difficulties of winter flying. Our visual environment, so critical to safe VFR flight, can also present some unique challenges during the winter season.

Ambient light levels, the light available to our eyes, glare, reduced visibility due to weather, and the various reflection and refraction illusions all affect our ability to see and respond to the world around us.

Many private pilots do not choose to give up flying or put their aircraft in storage for the winter. Commercial pilots and our dedicated cadre of flight instructors fly all year long. For them, it is a good plan to be aware of the various difficulties that conditions can produce and make decisions based on full knowledge of the effects of those conditions.

At all times it is important to know our personal limits and stick by them.

The ambient light level, the quantity of light available to our eyes, can have a significant effect on our ability to see. Human eyes have different sensitivity levels depending on available or ambient light level.

A quick review of our secondary school biology will remind us that there are two types of light receptors in the eye: rods and cones. Cones are concentrated near the centre of the eye, the fovea; rods are concentrated around the periphery.

Cones are the primary receptors for colour and visual acuity, recognition of detail; rods have no colour sensitivity, are poor at receiving specific detail, but are the primary receptors for the perception of motion. Under low light conditions, scotopic vision, rods provide the major source of visual information to the brain. Under bright light conditions, photopic vision, the cones predominate.

Lying between scotopic illumination levels and photopic illumination levels is the mesopic range, or mid-level lighting conditions where both cones and rods function well. In this light range, vision is both peripheral and central and colour begins to become clearly apparent.[2]

For sharp vision, photopic vision levels of light are required, and we must be looking directly at an object. In low light conditions, we cannot see an object as clearly looking directly at it. We must look a bit to the side to maximize our clarity. Averted vision is the best way to maximize the efficacy of the rods.[3]

According to Werner Adrian of the University of Waterloo, "With decreasing luminance levels, the spectral sensitivity of the eye changes... This goes in concert with the fading of colours until, in low levels, we perceive brightness only."[4]

As the light dims during a winter flight, it is an excellent idea to remember that our visual capabilities are changing as well. Direct vision is no longer as clear and precise as it would be in bright light conditions. As light levels decrease we begin to rely more and more on our peripheral vision and our sense of motion rather than our direct, detail vision. In low light situations, our scanning techniques—something about which we can make decisions—should reflect this new visual reality.

Glare, resulting from direct or reflected light, can also be a significant factor during winter months. Low sun angles tend to increase the amount of glare to which a pilot is exposed. The eye responds to glare physiologically by closing the retinal opening, decreasing the amount of light entering the eye. The normal, human response to painful glare is to either shade the eyes or to turn away from the glare source or both.

Each of these natural and necessary responses to the sudden brightness of glare significantly reduces a pilot's ability to see objects in proximity to the glare source. We have all experienced the difficulties involved in flying toward the sun when it is at a low angle or over flooded fields or snowy areas strongly reflecting the sun's glare. Any scratches or dirt on the windscreen magnify the effects of glare and make vision even more difficult.

Wearing a good pair of aviation approved sunglasses and doing a proper job of cleaning the aeroplane's windscreen before each flight are highly recommended and provide some level of mitigation.

It may sometimes be a very good plan to consider the sun's position when plotting a navigational route. Just as a sailboat might tack or zigzag into the wind, the pilot of an aircraft flying under Visual Flight Rules might consider adapting his or her route to avoid flying directly toward the sun.

Reduced visibility due to weather conditions needs little explanation, but it is an important phenomenon to keep in the front of our minds. Rain, snow, mist, cloud, drizzle, and ice fog all reduce our ability to see clearly, decrease the distance we are able to see, and reduce the ambient light level that also affects our vision as we discussed previously.

In extreme snow or cloud conditions or when the ground is completely covered with snow and the sky is clouded, we may experience whiteout during which we lose our ability to differentiate between sky and ground. Our horizon will disappear. Our depth perception and distance judgement will be lost. We are no longer flying VFR but have entered Instrument Meteorological Conditions, IMC.

In whiteout conditions, immediate transition to instruments is mandatory.

Landing in whiteout conditions or even conditions approaching whiteout will make judging approach height extremely difficult and will provide a visual environment similar to a glassy-water landing on floats without the benefit of a visible horizon.

Rain and drizzle also produce some interesting illusions. As light passes from one medium to another—air to water and back—its bends or "refracts" and spreads apart or "diffuses." Both these phenomenon can have serious consequences if not properly understood and compensated for.

All of us have, at one time or another, stuck our hand or a stick into water and seen the hand or stick "bend". This phenomenon is called refraction. Light passing through the medium of water changes direction giving the illusion that the immersed object is bent.

Refraction of light through the medium of water can result in our seeing objects outside at a different altitude than they would normally appear. The light arriving at our eyes has been bent en-route giving a false perception of our horizon.

Tops of obstacles like hills and the horizon itself will appear lower than they actually are. The general rule of thumb is that objects half a mile ahead of our aircraft may appear to be as much as 200 feet lower than actual.

The illusion in itself is not dangerous if it is understood to be an illusion. If we respond to conditions as though our perceived image is, in fact, reality, we could be in for a shocking surprise.

Refraction can produce some very interesting illusions on landing and taking off, as well. I always try to make a point of taking students up flying in the rain, at some point during their training, so they can see firsthand that the illusions we have been talking about in ground school are both very true and, at first encounter, confusing.

Light passing through water as well as being refracted is diffused or spread apart. This results in two interesting effects: lighted objects in the distance will appear less bright. The light emanative from a source is, essentially, broken up, diffused, lowering the apparent intensity. Our brain interprets the apparent lowered intensity of light from a source to mean the source is farther away than it actually is.

Lighted objects, such as runway lights, because of the diffusion of their light, will appear to be larger than they actually are; our poor little brains will be tempted to interpret this information to mean that the lights are closer than they actually are.

Winter can provide some of the most beautiful flying of the entire year. Aircraft perform much better in the cold dense air. When winter conditions are stable, summer's thermal turbulence—irritating at the best of times—is absent. Winter flying does, however, present a number of serious challenges to our skills and to our fund of knowledge.

Just as we must develop the knowledge, skills and judgement to deal safely and effectively with phenomenon such as ice, hail, wind, and slippery runways, so too, it is important to know and understand, to have the knowledge, skills, and judgement to deal with the unique visual effects of the winter season.

NOTES:

Chapter 4.4

Stress

"Ninety percent of this game is half mental."

-Yogi Berra

According to Transport Canada, stress is often a major contributing factor in aviation accidents. Stress is a difficult phenomenon to measure and quantify, except perhaps very indirectly through a measurement of the amount of adrenalin remaining in a post accident pilot's bloodstream, so it is often overlooked in accident reports.

We do know that nearly half the adults in North America suffer the adverse effects of stress, and that stress related complaints account for over 75% of all visits to the doctor.[5]

There is no doubt, however, that excess stress plays a significant role in the events preceding and leading up to aviation accidents, and that developing a working knowledge of what stress is, how to recognize stress in ourselves, how it affects our performance, and what we can do to control our stress levels can be of help in reducing the risks involved in flight.

Stress is actually a difficult concept to define in a precise way. Transport Canada uses the definition suggested by Miller and Smith, 1993: "Stress is the state of dynamic tension created when you respond to perceived demands and pressures from outside and from within yourself."

The key words in the definition direct us toward the concepts of dynamic tension, response to perceived demands, and pressures from both outside and from within. Stress is, essentially, a form of resistance to perceived demands, both external and internal: it is self-generated.

Outside or inside events do not cause stress; they can be, however, trigger mechanisms for our personal reactions.

All living beings experience some degree of stress, and a certain level of stress is, in fact, required to ensure a reasonable level of performance: the perceptions and responses required to deal effectively with our environment. An adequate level of dynamic tension between our environment and ourselves is necessary for successful interaction and response.

Different people respond differently to the same situations or stimuli. As Epictetus (55-135 A.D) said, "Men are disturbed not by things but by the views which they take of them." The exact same objective perception or event may elicit a very different response in one person than it does in another.

Each one of us operates at a different base level of stress, which changes from day to day, hour to hour. Each one of us has a history: a genetic makeup, a set of memories, hopes, fears, and expectations against which each new event or perception is measured and evaluated. Our response to each perceived demand, either internal or external, is the product of our measurement and evaluation against the background of our unique physical, mental, and emotional makeup.

For one person, getting a credit card bill in the mail might be a non-event, or, perhaps, a minor irritation. For another person, the same bill might send their blood pressure through the roof, elicit a state of panic, and leave them dysfunctional for the remainder of the day.

When flying, too low a stress level can be almost as dangerous as one that is too high. Our lowest level of stress occurs as we slide into sleep. A very low stress level can result in complacency, inattention, and neglect of required duties. Too high a stress level, particularly if that stress is prolonged, can result in exhaustion, serious errors in judgement, and an inability to function, both physically and mentally.

The Canadian Mental Health Association describes the "stress response", the sequence of events we experience when faced with a stress-producing situation, as a three-step process:

- **Stage 1**: Mobilizing Energy;
- **Stage 2**: Consuming Energy Stores; and
- **Stage 3**: Draining Energy Stores.

In **Stage 1** of the stress response process, the body perceives the stressor—the event or thought that triggers stress—and releases adrenaline. The heart and respiration rates increase. Our senses become more focused and sensitive; we become more perceptive and alert. Both positive and potentially dangerous events can trigger this first stage.

At this stage our performance is excellent. We are alert, focused, and yet still remain relatively relaxed and flexible. We are functioning, as we might say, at the top of our game.

Depending on our overall fitness level at onset, this stage can last for a considerable time, but there are limits. Fatigue develops, and our ability to maintain a high level of focus and function deteriorates. For most people, 2-3 hours is a reasonable limit to maintain a high level of focus and function in a demanding, vibrating, noisy environment like the cockpit of a small aircraft.

Some brave souls will tell you about their flights lasting 5-7 hours or even longer, but they are simply not functioning at the same level by the end of the flight as they were during the first few hours. This is one of the reasons that the descent, approach, and landing phases of flight account for 61% of all aviation accidents although they represent only 24% of the total exposure time during flight.

In **Stage 2**, the body begins to release stored sugars and fats to produce more available energy to meet the demands of an ongoing or more threatening stressful situation. The senses tend to become more narrowly focused, and they begin to exclude information that may not be evaluated as relevant to the immediate perceived threat. We may also begin to experience an increased level of anxiety, memory loss, and reduced ability to deal with more complex types of problems. Our ability to make sound judgments is becoming impaired.

Blood flow to the higher centres of the brain, the cerebral cortex, the portion of the brain responsible for processing complex mental activities such as thinking, remembering, perceiving, initiating voluntary movement, the mental home of decision-making and judgement, is reduced. Our performance level begins to deteriorate.

That old adage of being too scared to move has a solid physiological basis.

As the function of the cerebral cortex decreases, the limbic and cerebellum regions of the brain begin to take on a larger share of our total brain information processing functions. The limbic region, sometimes referred to as the mammalian brain, the "fight or flight" centre of the brain, whose major functions include control of emotions and the carrying out of routine sequential activities, begins to take more of a front seat in how we operate.

It is interesting to know that the three major regions of the brain, the cerebral cortex, the limbic region, and the cerebellum each have independent access to sensory input data and muscle response mechanisms. If you put your hand on a hot stove the cerebellum, the region that controls such functions as balance, muscular coordination, heart rate, respiration rate, and automatic responses can respond much faster than the two higher regions and without the need for conscious thought, forcing you to remove your hand from the perceived threat. It is not a region of the brain, however, capable of making reasoned judgments.

The limbic region of the brain might be the first to respond to someone raising his hand in anger, posing a potential threat, without having to reference all those conflict resolution courses you took on how to deal with angry people. That knowledge and those patterns of interaction will be resting comfortably in the cerebral cortex, put effectively on hold until the level of stress resulting from the situation is reduced.

If Stage 2 continues for too long a period of time or the perceived threat is too powerful, we progress into **Stage 3** of the stress response sequence.

In Stage 3, our body's need for energy becomes greater that our ability to provide it. Our ability to respond in a meaningful way to our environment and our own thoughts deteriorates rapidly. Making sound judgments or solving complex problems becomes extremely difficult. We may still be able to perform uncomplicated routine tasks, but it will become impossible to respond effectively in an intelligent manner to unexpected or difficult situations.

Too much stress or too prolonged a period of stress renders each one of us dysfunctional and unsafe to pilot an aircraft.

Stress, beyond a certain point, is not a performance enhancer.

Recognizing our own personal stress levels can be a complex problem, particularly if we allow the stress response sequence to progress too far. If we fail to recognize and take positive steps to control an increasing stress level, we move toward stress levels where the judgments and the problem solving capabilities we need to make reasonable and intelligent decisions about how to handle a difficult situation degrade.

Each one of us will respond to stress in our own unique manner, and it is important to monitor and become familiar with our own individual patterns. Some typical symptoms of increasing stress that are easily observed are:

1. An increase in heart and respiration rates;
2. Increased muscle tension;
3. Rushed speech;
4. A sense of impatience;
5. Increasingly mechanical responses;
6. Irritability; and
7. A tendency to focus on smaller aspects of a situation.

Gaining a familiarity with our own stress responses can be extremely helpful. If we can learn to recognize and take positive steps to reduce excess stress, we will be more able to maintain a high level of function in a difficult environment.

Deep breathing, taking a short break, and focusing on standard procedures can all be extremely helpful in times of stress. There is an old tradition in the British Navy: regardless of the impending crisis, the captain always takes a moment to put on his hat before responding. He takes a moment for a breath and to collect his thoughts before engaging in the process of sorting out a difficult situation.

As with all human factors, successfully dealing with stress requires awareness, attitude, knowledge, and discipline. We must be aware of our personal stress levels and their patterns, be familiar with our personal stress response symptoms, and know the specific triggers that tend to increase or reduce our level of stress responses.

Developing a proper attitude about stress and its importance, in terms of our actual capacity to deal effectively with the conditions we may encounter during a particular flight, is also critical. The correct attitude toward safety directs us to respond in a positive manner to any signs of potential, developing problems.

Knowledge is a very necessary part of the solution. We must know and understand what stress is, how it operates, both theoretically and personally, and what we can do to maximize its benefits and minimize its negative effects. Discipline provides the voice and practice to "do the right thing" each and every time. Without the required discipline to do the right thing each and every time, we leave ourselves and our passengers vulnerable and unprotected from the potentially negative effects of stress.

A high stress level in the pilot is no less dangerous that a loss of oil pressure.

Knowledge, without discipline, awareness, and the proper attitude does not carry the ball to the goal line. It is the combination of all four elements that allows us to minimize and manage risk.

Stress is something that affects each and every one of us. It can be either our best friend or our worst enemy, depending on our ability to recognize and effectively respond to our personal stress levels on an ongoing basis. Just as one might monitor temperature, oil pressure, and fuel gauges during a flight, so too, pilot stress levels should be on the list of monitored elements contributing to a safe flight.

NOTES:

Chapter 4.5

The Four Keys: Knowledge, Awareness, Attitude and Discipline

"Always bear in mind that your own resolution to succeed is more important than any other."

-Abraham Lincoln

There is a grassy area bordering on the transient aircraft day parking area here at Chilliwack (CYCW). Right at the edge of the tarmac, the ground drops into a shallow ditch. I have seen a number of people push their aircraft back off the tarmac to be out of the way only to find, when they are ready to leave, they cannot push the plane back on to the hard surface.

An older gentleman found himself in just such a position a week or so back. I was inside working with a student when I noticed the man struggling with his aircraft. Without a word or hesitation, two younger fellows who had just parked their plane walked over, positioned themselves one behind each strut, and provided the needed extra human power to solve the problem.

On the other hand, I had the opportunity to watch as a fellow instructor sat in the cockpit while his student warmed up a twin aircraft right in front of the terminal doorway, blowing bark mulch and other debris all over the walkways and up to the doorway itself. When a passenger waiting for his charter flight walked out to alert the instructor to the havoc he was creating, the instructor simply waved him off.

According to Transport Canada, as of the year 2012, there were a total of 50,721 licenced pilots in Canada, including both helicopter and aeroplane: 7972 Commercial Pilots, 25,868 Private Pilots, and 12,192 Airline Transport Licenced pilots: about 0.2% of the population.[6]

We are a small community.

Being a small community, I would like to suggest it is important to respect one another, all of the non-aviation people we affect daily, and work together, as best we may, to continue to create a positive, working community, a community that helps itself whenever possible and is aware and conscious of its actions and how those actions affect others.

Each time we participate in a conversation about aviation, visit an airport, or take an aircraft flying we have an opportunity to help or harm the aviation industry. No matter how alone you may feel sitting in the cockpit of your aircraft, you are not. You are out there, on display in a public forum, representing all of us who take to the skies.

In training programs we often speak of the four keys to successful practice: knowledge, awareness, attitude, and discipline. For the most part, these are spoken of in reference to flight and the flying environment. I would like to suggest their application is, in fact, more broadly based.

Knowledge is defined as the, "...body of information, facts, and procedures that needs to be known."[7] Knowing what you need to know as a pilot does not end with an understanding of aerodynamics, meteorology, and air law. I would suggest knowledge of how others are affected by your words and actions is also critical.

Maintaining awareness of what you are doing and how that impacts others is always important. This applies in the air and on the ground, both in terms of safe flying and in terms of the image you portray of aviation. Being aware of the effects of your actions is a part of the total responsibility of holding an aviation licence.

Think of the two cases presented in the opening paragraphs of this article. Both of these events were witnessed by the people sitting in the airport coffee shop and those sitting in the terminal building at that moment. Both of the incidents revealed important information about aviation. Which image would you choose for people to carry away? Which image would you choose for people to be holding when airport closures are being suggested, when government legislation affecting aviation is working its way toward enactment?

The attitude you take with you into the cockpit is critical to how well you manage the risks involved in flight. The attitude you portray to others when speaking about flying or exercising your licence privileges sends a clear message into the world about aviation. Remember, you are the 'expert' to many of your friends and acquaintances; anytime you are acting in the capacity of a pilot you represent all of us.

Discipline is the last key and is a very foundational one. It represents the consistency we all need to practice both in the air and on the ground. The disciplined part of us is the part that says, "Do it right even if no one is watching or listening." It is the part of us that demands we use our knowledge, remain focused and aware, monitor our attitudes and behaviours, and attend to that which requires attention.

As a holder of an aviation licence or as a student working towards one, you are a part of the aviation community. In the air and on the ground you represent that community and present a picture and image of it to the people with whom you interact and with the people who observe you in your interactions.

What aviation is and will be in Canada is, in large part, a reflection of those of us who make up the community of people involved in aviation. Ensuring you are knowledgeable, aware, develop and demonstrate positive attitudes, and remain disciplined in your approach to aviation serves all of us and helps create the background, the human infrastructure, which ensures positive growth and a supportive environment for the industry at large.

NOTES:

Chapter 4.6

Assessing Positive Flying Practices

"Possessing the proper mental attitude towards piloting an aeroplane is the prime factor governing safe flying..."

-From the Ground Up

We all know the vast majority of aviation accidents are the product of human decisions. Even accidents involving mechanical failure are often compounded by human error or poor decision-making. The attitude we bring to flying plays a critical role in how safe we are, or, as Adam Hunt of COPA points out, how well we manage the risks involved in flying. Learning to assess the particular constellation of attitudes we carry with us as we climb into the cockpit can be a very useful tool in helping us be the best pilot it is in us to be.

Just as we us a checklist to prepare an aircraft for flight, we can also use a checklist to assess our own readiness to take on the responsibilities of Pilot in Command. Let's take a look at some of the behaviours indicative of positive attitude as suggested in the *Human Factors for Aviation, Instructor's Guide.*

As you go through the list, be honest with yourself; see how you are doing in each area; think about how you might find some room for improvement, however small. In the end, how safe we all are is a direct function of how safe each one of us is. You might want to try out the following rating scale for each item:

- 4 indicates always;
- 3 indicates usually;
- 2 indicates sometimes; and
- 1 indicates infrequently or never.

A pilot with good flying practices demonstrates a positive attitude by:

1. **Following SOPs and procedures**. This seems simple enough, but it takes a certain amount of discipline. Following SOPs and procedures means simply what it says. We want to get into the habit of doing the right things from beginning to end: checking weather and NOTAMS, using checklists, performing thorough

pre-flight inspections, carefully ensuring the area is clear before starting the engine, carrying out careful lookouts during flight. We want it to be second nature to complete all the hundreds of little details that go into minimizing the risks involved in flight.

2. If you don't have a set of SOPs for yourself, you might want to take a look at developing some. Talk it over with a professional pilot, if you know one. Your aircraft's POH, the Flight Training Manual, and your AIP are all excellent reference materials. Have a chat with your favourite instructor. Just the process of thinking it all through can lead to a positive change.

3. **Setting a good example.** This means doing the right thing even when no one is watching. When people are watching, setting a good example becomes very important. Many folks take their clues from what others do. One person consistently doing the right thing can encourage many others to follow suit.

Dave English, in his little book, *Slipping the Surly Bonds,*[8] includes the anonymous quote, "Whenever we talk about a pilot who has been killed in a flying accident, we should all keep one thing in mind: "Every instructor, supervisor, and contemporary who ever spoke to him [or her] had an opportunity to influence his or her judgement, so a little bit of all of us goes with every pilot we lose."

It is a unique and very important opportunity we have to influence the behaviour of others by always trying to set the best personal example we can.

Setting high standards for yourself. I have this discussion with myself and with my students on a regular basis. Proficient flying skills do not, as it were, drop from the sky. They are built moment to moment through being consistent, paying attention, and not being willing to accept second best.

Setting a high standard of performance for yourself builds towards excellence. If you set out to fly at 2000', make it 2000' not 1950' or 2050'. Make each turn the best you can manage, each takeoff, each landing. As an old "friend" said to me once, "Aim low, hit low." The opposite is also true. If we want to achieve a high standard, that's the standard we want to set for ourselves.

Maintaining currency. Maintaining currency is, of course, a legal requirement. More than that, however, it is making a personal decision about maintaining a level of proficiency you need to be both safe and comfortable in an aircraft. We all know that skills decay without use. The key question here is: am I up to my own level as well as the legal minimum?

Flying within current proficiency level. This item pretty well speaks for itself. We all need to be clear about what we can and can't do, our actual experience level, how good we really are. Just because the VFR rules say below 1000' in daytime, 2 miles flight visibility (aeroplanes) and clear of cloud is sufficient doesn't mean that's good enough for a particular pilot on a particular day. This is where our judgement needs to be alive, well, and tuned in to our own personal proficiency level.

Self-evaluating. I like to think this is something I do regularly and continuously. And, indeed, here we are working through a self-evaluation at this moment. It's the ongoing process of looking at what we do, evaluating it, determining what could be improved, making a plan to improve it, and carrying out the plan. This is how we grow: little by little, but constantly.

So, let's add up our score and see how we are doing. A score of 24 is excellent. You certainly don't need to show anyone else the results of your self-evaluation, but if you are coming in with a score less than 21 you might want to give some thought to the standards you are setting for yourself. Flying is one of the most exciting and involving activities, but it is a very unforgiving one.

To a great extent, the attitude we take with us into the air is a significant factor in determining how safe a pilot we are, how well we are managing the inherent risks involved in flight. Attitudes, of course, are difficult to monitor and evaluate directly, but we can monitor and evaluate our behaviours.

If you can truly say, after taking the little inventory above, that your behaviours reflect a positive attitude, good for you! You are doing your part to reduce and manage the risks of flying both for yourself and for all the rest of us. Keep up the good work.

NOTES:

Chapter 4.6.1

ASSESSMENT OF PILOTING ATTITUDES SELF EVALUATION FORM

Name: _____

Date: _____

Total Score: _____

Scoring:

4 indicates always;

3 indicates usually;

2 indicates sometimes; and

1 indicates infrequently or never.

___I follow SOPs and procedures every time I fly.

___I set a good example for others at all times.

___I set high standards for myself on every flight.

___I confirm and maintain currency prior to each flight.

___I fly within my current proficiency level at all times.

___I self-evaluate after each flight.

_____ Total Score

Notes: Three things I could do to improve my piloting attitudes and actions over the next month:

1.

2.

3.

Chapter 4.7

Pilot Behaviours

"Any man who would worry about snakes might as well walk."
-W.F. Call

Piloting an aircraft requires the application of human behaviours to achieve a goal: safe and efficient flight. We can think of piloting behaviours as falling into three basic categories or behaviour sets: **skill-based behaviours, rules-based behaviours** and **knowledge-based behaviours.**[9]

Each of these behaviour sets encompasses both strengths and weaknesses.

Developing an understanding of and appreciation for the strengths and weaknesses of each set of behaviours can assist in providing a strong basis for informed decision-making when operating an aircraft.

Skill-based behaviours are most often the first type of behaviours encountered when a pilot-to-be begins his or her training. Coordination of rudder and aileron, use of pitch and power to maintain altitude and airspeed or rate of decent or climb, and maintaining correct visual references during a manoeuvre are all examples of skill-based behaviours. In order to successfully fly an aircraft a candidate for a pilot licence must develop, internalize and be able to demonstrate basic, required skills.

Particularly during the early stages of training, and perhaps as an ongoing commitment to maintaining or developing proficiency, skill-based behaviours are a significant focus for pilots. Developing at least basic proficiency in the necessary skills is both necessary and important in order to fly an aircraft.

As skills are developed and internalized, they require less and less conscious thought; they tend to become increasingly automatic, to habituate. As our skills progress we find we can apply carburetor heat, reduce power, adjust prop settings, set flaps, turn from downwind to base, talk on the radio, and still have enough consciousness left over to wonder whether we will be able to land, tie down, and make it home in time to watch the game on TV.

The more we practice a particular skill the more deeply habituated it becomes, making it increasingly difficult to change the particular pattern of movements and perceptions required to perform that skill. This is why re-learning a skill improperly taught is so very challenging. Once a pattern has become habituated, reversing the process is a steep uphill battle.

This is both the strength and weakness of skill-based behaviours.

A skill is simply a learned level of proficiency at performing a given task. It's like being very good at cutting with a knife. We can expertly cut vegetables for dinner or slice off a finger. The skill is the same. A decision must be made when and where to apply a particular skill. The fact that skills-based behaviours do tend to become habituated and automatic may lead us into precisely applying the wrong skill for current conditions. We could perform a perfectly executed turn into a hillside, for example.

A very skilled pilot is not necessarily a safe or efficient pilot. Piloting an aircraft requires more than skills, regardless of how finely honed those skills may be.

Stress, fatigue, preoccupation, or a new and unfamiliar environment can sufficiently distract a pilot from applying the correct skill for a particular situation. More than one retractable gear aircraft has landed gear up, not because there is a lack of skill on the part of the pilot but because there was a failure to apply the correct skills at the correct moment. Not too long ago the pilots of a commuter jet executed a skilful takeoff procedure on the wrong runway only to discover the runway was too short to achieve sufficient altitude to avoid encountering the disaster waiting ahead.

How many times have you driven home after work only to realize you have no recollection at all of the ride? You were operating on automatic; you were applying habituated skills with little or no conscious thought.

Relying on skill alone without the appropriate framework for judgments to guide those skills can be extremely hazardous. Allowing finely honed skills to become the sole basis of our flying practice can set the stage for extremely poor outcomes.

Rules-based behaviours are behaviours for which a routine or procedure has been developed and learned by the pilot. Using checklists or Standard Operating Procedures (SOP's) are excellent examples of rules-based behaviours.

A focus on rules based behaviours allows even moderately skilled pilots to operate aircraft both safely and efficiently in most situations and environments.

Rules-based behaviours are not necessarily behaviours that must be memorized or internalized, as are skills-based behaviours; they are behaviours whose "rules" or "procedures" are memorized. For example, what the pilot must know regarding the activities for dealing with a pre-flight inspection, the pre-takeoff procedures, or an engine fire in flight is that he or she must make use of a standardized checklist or procedure. The key focus of rules-based behaviours is the focus on standardized procedures: red light number 3 on: switch 4 to position 2.

Rules-based behaviours provide a tried and true framework for the application of skills.

Rules-based behaviours are typically based on long developed and tested knowledge and experience. The history of errors and successes resulting from years of experience form the basis for procedures designed to prevent future errors and guide future successes. As the saying goes, "You never live long enough to make all the mistakes yourself, so learn from the mistakes of others."

Rules-based behaviours are strongly emphasized in commercial operations and pilot training for excellent reasons. When flying in a multi-crew environment, for example, unless standardized procedures are established and followed, chaos would soon result. What actions are taken, the order in which they are accomplished, and even the communications between crewmembers are all highly structured and standardized. This assists greatly in assuring an efficient and safe flight.

The potential weakness when operating under a rules-based behaviour system occurs when there is an initial misdiagnosis of a problem or situation, and the wrong procedure is applied. The successful implementation of rules-based behaviours requires sufficient skill-based behaviours and the required knowledge to know when particular procedures should be applied.

The third category of behaviours, **knowledge-based behaviours**, apply in situations where a decision must be made regarding which specific rule must be applied or when no specific procedure has been established. We move, here, into the realm of conscious decision-making, relying on our own personal knowledge and experience to deal with particular situations.

While knowledge-based solutions may appear to be, in a sense, the highest form of problem solving, these behaviours are subject to a wide range of human errors.

Getting creative in a difficult situation can all too often lead to making a situation worse rather than better. More than one light aircraft has gone down when the pilot applied carburetor heat to deal with a faltering engine and then decided because the initial problem appeared to worsen to adjust the carburetor heat back to cold rather than follow the accepted procedure of leaving carburetor heat hot, increasing power, and leaning the mixture appropriately until the problem disappears or further diagnosis is indicated.

At any given moment we only know what we know; we don't know what we don't know. Even the most experienced pilots have limits to the depth and breadth of their knowledge and experience.

One of the basic characteristics of human thought is to structure information and make inferences from that structure. This structuring process tends to occur very early in process of assessing a situation. Once we have created a structure for the information we have available, it becomes extremely difficult to change or re-structure the framework we have created. We tend very quickly, in a problem solving situation, to exclude new information or information that contradicts the structure we have developed in the very early stages of the process. Remember the old saying, "Don't confuse me with the facts; my mind is already made up"?

People all hold a plethora of hopes, fears and wishes. These, as well, tend to colour and format how we process information. It is extremely difficult to remain neutral about information in a difficult problem-solving situation. Even negative information, information that would indicate a flaw in our structure and assumptions, tends to be disregarded or ignored once we have allowed our tendency to seek a solution to gain momentum.

A classic example: "I know those clouds will clear and the ceiling will lift as I get closer to home."

Stress and distraction only make things worse. Excessive stress is not a performance enhancer. Problems we might easily solve, given time and leisure on the ground, become a breeding ground for disaster in an environment with increasing pressure, limited time, and a heightened stress level. It's often fairly simple, given time, full knowledge, and leisure to analyze the cause or causes of an accident after the fact, but we weren't sitting in the cockpit just before the event.

Relying on knowledge and experience alone puts our eggs in a very fragile basket, even more so for pilots lacking the advantage of extensive knowledge and experience.

The process of becoming a competent, safe, and efficient pilot as opposed to someone who flies an aircraft, relies on all three types of behaviour sets: **skill-based, rule-based and knowledge-based.**

Each set of behaviours must be developed and applied appropriately and in the correct combination to allow us to successfully carry out the duties required of an aircraft pilot.

The focus and discipline of using rules-based behaviours provides the most solid framework to integrate and apply both skill-based and knowledge-based behaviours. Without skills, it is impossible to successfully fly and aircraft; without knowledge it becomes extremely difficult to select the correct procedure to apply under various conditions. But, without the foundation of rules-based behaviours, we are essentially "making it up as we go", opening ourselves to an all too wide variety of potential hazards.

As they say, "If all else fails, read the instructions." Following standard procedures, the tested product of time and experience, is the solid foundation on which to build a long and safe career as a pilot.

Enjoy.

NOTES:

Chapter 4.8

Situational Awareness

"An expert is someone who has succeeded in making decisions and judgments simpler through knowing what to pay attention to and what to ignore."

-Edward de Bono

Pilot error has been found to be a "broad cause factor" in 84% of all aviation accidents and 96% of fatal accidents.[10] Research developed by the Australian Transportation Safety Board (ASTB) indicates approximately 85% of incident and accident reports mention loss of situational awareness as a contributing factor. In aviation, maintaining a high level of situation awareness (SA) is one of the most critical and challenging features of a pilot's job.[11]

Aviation accidents and incidents are virtually never single cause events. In recognition of this reality, accident and incident reports include analysis of Findings as to Causes, Contributing Factors, and often include Findings as to Risk; all of these factors combine to produce the unwanted result: an incident or accident. As our understanding of the dynamics of unwanted consequences deepens, more and more attention is being paid to the role of situational awareness as a contributing factor in aviation accidents and incidents.

As Table 1 demonstrates, degraded or poor situational awareness can lead to inadequate decision-making and inappropriate actions on the part of pilots.[12]

Factor	% of Events
Inadequate decision-making	74%
Omission of action or inappropriate action	72%
Non-adherence to criteria for stabilized approach	66%
Inadequate crew coordination, cross-check and back-up	63%
Insufficient horizontal or vertical Situational Awareness	52%
Inadequate or insufficient understanding of prevailing conditions	48%
Slow or delayed action	45%
Flight handling difficulties	45%
Deliberate non-adherence to procedures	40%
Inadequate training	37%
Incorrect or incomplete pilot/controller communication	33%
Interaction with automation	20%

**Table 1: Causal Factors in Approach and Landing Accidents
Source: Flight Safety Foundation – Flight Safety Digest Volume 17 &
18 – November 1988/February 1999**

Table 1 shows us that two factors, inadequate decision-making and omission or inappropriate actions, occurred in 74% and 72% of the approach and landing accidents analyzed by the ATSB, respectively. Both inadequate decision-making and omission or inappropriate actions can easily result from loss of the pilot's situational awareness. If a pilot is not quite sure what is going on, it is very difficult for him or her to make wise decisions or perform skilful and appropriate actions.

What is situational awareness? It is defined as having an accurate perception and understanding of what is happening around you combined with a clear picture of what is likely to occur in the near future.

Military and police literature often refer to good situational awareness as having a "360 degree mindset". It is a term used as a reminder that our world is spherical rather than linear, evolving rather than static: our environment includes inside and outside, above, level, below, both sides, in front, and behind, all of which change with time. Situational awareness is what Gonzales refers to as, "…paying attention to your surroundings…."[13]

A useful model of situational awareness divides the activities involved into three components: perception of what is happening, Level 1 SA; understanding what has been perceived, Level 2 SA; and using what is understood to think ahead into the future, Level 3 SA.

Level 1 SA, perception, is gathering the information to build a mental model of the ambient environment, using our senses to form a picture of current conditions. For a pilot, the current environment includes the machine we are flying, the environment in which that flight is taking place, and his or her own condition.

We all operate with limits on our attention and perception. A critical aspect of perception is the ability to prioritize what is important, what is relevant, and what, perhaps, poses an immediate or developing threat. Inexperience, reduced ability to pay attention, and time available all reduce and limit the clarity of the mental picture we have and to which we can apply our understanding and experience. If I never look at a fuel gauge, it will be difficult to factor fuel availability into my information base. If my scan includes only the front view, it will be very easy for me to miss aircraft or other objects approaching from abeam.

Fatigue and distraction are two significant perceptual reduction factors and have received increasing attention in the aviation community over the past few years. Attempting VFR flight in instrument meteorological conditions is one of the most consistently lethal mistakes in all of aviation.[14] Once outside visual reference is lost, our ability to form a useful mental picture of our environment is sadly reduced. If we don't or can't get the information we need, situational awareness is significantly reduced.

Level 2 SA, understanding, is the process of combining observations and perceptions from the real world with our training, knowledge, and experience to develop a mental model of our developing environment and situation. We are asking ourselves in an ongoing way, "What does all this mean?" We need the facts—the building blocks of our mental picture—but we must interpret those facts and assemble them into an understandable model if we are to make wise and successful decisions.

Level 3 SA, projection, is the process of extending our current mental picture into the future. This is a critical step toward wise decision-making and the basis for skilful action. Decisions and actions can only be taken in the current moment. What actions we take at a given moment depend largely on our assessment of what will unfold based on our perception and understanding of current conditions.

We all remember the story of the man falling from a ten story building who was asked, as he passed the fifth floor, "So, how's it going?" He replied, "So far, so good." Unless we are able to project our current model into the future in a timely and coherent manner, it is very difficult to make wise decisions and take skilful and appropriate actions to prevent unwanted consequences. Even in a light aeroplane traveling at moderate speed, two miles of distance from a potential threat can disappear in a minute or even less.

"Apathy, complacency, and denial are the three primary barriers to good situational awareness."[15]

While the accident rates for commercial, airline, and military flight operations have been steadily dropping, the accident rate for General Aviation has remained unacceptably high.

According to the most recent Transportation Safety Board's summary report of aviation accidents in Canada (2009), general aviation flying continues to show the highest rate of accidents and fatalities for any category of flight activity. Private pilots, over the last ten years, recorded a rate of 20.3 accidents/100,000 hours flown compared with the airlines which recorded an accident rate of only 0.1/100,000 hours flown.[16]

According to the NTSB, "Each year, hundreds of people — 450 in 2010 — are killed in GA accidents, and thousands more are injured. GA continues to have the highest aviation accident rates within civil aviation: about 6 times higher than small commuter and air taxi operations and over 40 times higher than larger transport category operations. Perhaps what is most distressing is that the causes of GA accidents are almost always a repeat of the circumstances of previous accidents."[17]

We have a clear picture of pilots most at risk to be one of these GA accident statistics:

The pilots most likely to have an accident:

1. Are between 35 and 39 years old;
2. Have between 100 and 500 hours total time;
3. Are on a personal flight; and
4. Are in visual flight conditions (VMC)

The most dangerous times in any pilot's career seem to occur at two, specific points:

1. When he or she has about 50 hours flying after earning his or her private pilot licence; and
2. When he or she has accumulated between 50 and 100 hours after earning an instrument rating.

To earn a licence or rating, a candidate must demonstrate he or she has achieved an acceptable level of skills, knowledge, and experience. Flight skills are developed during training and solo practice and then tested against a standard on a candidate's flight test.

Knowledge is developed through ground school, pre-flight briefings, and study; it is tested during the ground portion of a flight test and on the appropriate written exam.

Experience is measured by "time on task", flight hours accumulated during training and solo practice.

It is relatively easy to teach and measure skills. It is somewhat more difficult to teach or, more accurately, create an environment when developing knowledge is likely, and measuring knowledge is less certain than measuring skill level. Written and oral examinations, of necessity, sample knowledge and are limited in time and scope to within fairly well defined limits. In depth understanding is not likely to be accurately measured using a multiple choice exam format.

Providing training to increase the less tangible aspects of piloting, situational awareness for example, is a much more challenging exercise; and, as Ericsson and Charness noted in their1994 study, "Expert performance: it's structure and acquisition", many years of dedicated practice are necessary to achieve world-class expertise in any field. Most people do not deliberately practice after attaining minimal skill at some activity; they play for fun, not for keeps.[18]

It is important, however, to find entry points and places to begin. In their 2000 paper, "Pilot Situation Awareness Training in General Aviation", Mica Endsley and colleagues suggest four specific areas where additional training can increase and improve situational awareness in the general aviation pilot population:[19]

1. Task management;
2. Development of comprehension;
3. Projection and planning; and
4. Information seeking and self-checking activities

Task Management: Good task management skills and strategies appear to be a crucial factor in dealing with problems or potential problems. The best performing pilots facing non-normal situations have been found to employ management strategies based on the perceived severity of required tasks and situations.[20] Pilots who actively manage tasks and information are much less likely to find themselves in situations where they are overloaded and miss critical information.

Development of Comprehension: Learning to assess the temporal aspects of a situation, the risk levels involved and both the personal and system capabilities of the pilot and the machine, increase the ability of pilots to deal with non-normal situations. Practice in these aspects — how much time do I have, how bad is my situation, and what are my options for a successful outcome — all increase a pilot's ability to manage safe outcomes. A pilot caught in rising terrain that knows intimately the climb performance of his or her machine will be in a much better position to make wise decisions than the pilot who is guessing or hoping he or she might be able to climb over the hill.

Projection of Planning: Experienced and successful pilots appear to spend a significant time in pre-planning, information gathering, and actively engaging in contingency planning for flights. Practice with detailed and careful planning prior to flights and an exploration of possible contingencies considerably enhances a pilot's ability to successfully deal with what may occur during the course of a flight. Emphasis on options can be extremely helpful; things do not always progress as we hoped. The old adage, "Always leave yourself a way out," is a good one to keep handy.

Information Seeking and Self-Checking Activities: Pilots who make a habit of actively seeking out critical information are much more successful at making quicker adjustments and noticing trends as they develop. Emphasis on checking and validating assessments of the ambient situation has proven to increase the effectiveness of dealing with false expectations and incorrect mental models. Using the old "Devil's Advocate" strategy to question conclusions has been shown to be very effective.[21]

While training beyond the basic level required to earn a licence or rating is looked upon as an expensive and time consuming project by many general aviation pilots; the numbers don't lie. The accident and incident rate for GA flying continues to produce unacceptably high numbers. The FAA has listed GA accident rates as one of the specific items identified in their top 10 safety concerns.

The mandate is there for those in the flight training community to organize and provide ongoing training in specific areas, including situational awareness training, to help pilots toward increased proficiency and safety.

As the old saying goes, "If you think safety is expensive try an accident."

NOTES:

(Endnotes)

1 Kershner, William, The Advanced Pilot's Flight Manual sixth Edition, Iowa State University Press, 1994

2 Crawford, David, 1998, Some Issues in Low Light Level Vision, IDA Inc., Tucson, Arizona, pg. 1

3 Crawford, David, 1998, Some Issues in Low Light Level Vision, IDA Inc., Tucson, Arizona, pg. 1

4 Adrian, Werner, 1997, The Influence of the Spectral Power Distribution for Equal Visual Performance in Roadway Light Levels. Paper given at the International Lighting Conference in Durban, South Africa, September 1997.

5 Transport Canada, TP12863 (E), Human Factors for Aviation -- Basic Handbook, pg 107.

6 http://www.tc.gc.ca/eng/civilaviation/standards/general-personnel-stats-stats-2300.htm

7 Transport Canada, Human Factors for Aviation, Instructor's Guide, TP 12865 (E), Transport Canada Safety and Security, Ottawa, Ontario

8 English, David, Slipping the Surly Bonds: Great Quotations on Flight, McGraw-Hill Publishing, 1998, ISBN 0070220166

9 For more detailed information reference TP 12863(E), Human Factors for Aviation, Basic Handbook

10 Transport Canada, Human Factors for Aviation, Basic Handbook, pg. 3

11 Endsley, Mica R., and Michelle M. Robertson, "Training for Situation Awareness", Ednsley, M.R. and Garland, D.J. (eds) (2000) Situation Awareness Analysis and Measurement. Mahwak, NJ: Lawrence Erlbaum Associates.

12 http://www.airbus.com/fileadmin/media_gallery/files/safety_library_items/AirbusSafetyLib_-FLT_OPS-HUM_PER-SEQ06.pdf

13 Gonzalez, J. (2004). Situational Awareness. SWAT, January, 18-20.

14 http://www.aopa.org/asf/ntsb/vfrintoimc.cfm

15 http://www.personalsafetygroup.com/about/situational-awareness-training/

16 Transportation Safety Board of Canada, Statistical Summary Aviation Occurrences 2009

17 http://www.ntsb.gov/safety/mwl-2.html2

18 Ericsson, K.A. & Charness, N. (1994). Expert performance: Its structure and acquisition. American Psychologist, 49, 725-747.

19 Endsley, Mica et all, "Pilot Situation Awareness Training in General Aviation", Proceedings of the 14th triennial Congress of the International Ergonomics Association and the 44th annual meeting of the Human Factors and Ergonomics Society, 2000.

20 Schutte, P.C. and Trujillo, A.C., (1996) "Flight crew task management in non-normal situations," Proceedings of the Human Factors and Ergonomics Society 40th Annual Meeting (pp 244-249) Santa Monica, California.

21 Klein, G. (1995, November) "Studying situation awareness in the context of decision-making incidents," Paper presented at the Experimental Analysis and Measurement of Situation Awareness, Daytona Beach, FL.

PART 5: AVIATION SAFETY

Chapter 5.1

Aviation Accidents

"Pilot error is an action or decision of the pilot that, if not caught and corrected, could contribute to the occurrence of an accident or incident. Inaction and indecision are included in the definition."

-ICAO

Aviation accident statistics developed by the Canadian Transportation Safety Board (TSB) and in the United States by the National Transportation Safety Board (NTSB) show we have a typical "good news/bad news" situation.

The "good news" is that since the end of WWII both the accident rates and the fatal accident rates have steadily fallen. The "bad news" is that we still have accidents, both fatal and non-fatal. According to Transport Canada, the current rate of aviation accidents in Canada is about 13 per 100,000 hours flown; fewer than 2 fatal accidents occur per 100,000 hours flown.[1]

Pilot error was found to be a "broad cause/factor" in 84% of all accidents and 96% of fatal accidents. Modern aircraft maintained to modern standards are quite reliable. The most difficult part of the equation to work with continues to be, as they used to say, "the nut that holds the steering wheel."

Accident statistics indicate that 'descent, approach, and landing' are the most dangerous phases of flight followed by 'take-off and climb.' While descent, approach, and landing accounts for only 24% of exposure time, it results in 61% of all accidents. Cruise flight accounts for 60% of total exposure time, but results in fewer than 17% of accidents.[2]

When a pilot's workload is high, as on approach and landing, accident rates increase. Approach also occurs at the end of a flight when a pilot is most fatigued. High workload coupled with greater fatigue level.... you do the math. No big surprises here.

Work with pilot statistics shows a number of identifiable patterns.[3] The pilots most likely to have an accident:

1. Are between 35 and 39 years old;
2. Have between 100 and 500 hours total time;
3. Are on a personal flight; and
4. Are in visual flight conditions (VMC)

The most dangerous times in any pilot's career seem to occur at two, specific points:

1. When he or she has about 50 hours flying after earning his or her private pilot licence; and
2. When he or she has accumulated between 50 and 100 hours after earning an instrument rating.

The key common factors appear to be that a pilot's confidence at these critical times exceeds his or her competence. Pilots may unknowingly put themselves in situations beyond their capabilities; they have not developed the necessary experience to recognize the level of danger involved. Many weather-related accidents fall into this category.

Another pattern to be aware of is that, in the normal course of events, as pilots increase their exposure to risk, they are more likely to encounter dangerous situations.

During flight training, pilot candidates fly under the watchful eye of instructors and within a tightly regulated regimen. Their judgement is monitored; direction and feedback are always available. The likelihood of setting out into marginal weather or into a situation beyond a pilot's abilities is very limited.

Immediately following flight training, pilots with a new licence will typically be very conscious of their developing skill levels, their lack of experience, and will regulate their decisions based on that sense of inexperience. They are likely to seek help and advice from more experienced pilots.

As pilots gain experience, they begin to develop a sense of confidence and will begin to venture further and further into new situations. This is a very positive trend and, if done within reasonable limits, leads to pilots acquiring the needed experience to become good aviators.

We all know experience is a product of time on task. You cannot gain experience from any source other than doing the job. Knowledge, and sometimes insight, can be passed along from one person to another, but only each individual person gains experience through the process of doing.

Confidence and experience develop separately and at their own rates. The most vulnerable moments are when our confidence has developed faster than our competence, and we "feel" more capable than we actually are.

Of course, experienced pilots have accidents, too. Sometimes very experienced pilots have accidents. None of us is immune to making mistakes, experiencing lapses in judgement, or misinterpreting events or perceptions. And rarely, machines do fail.

Our biggest enemy is always that moment of overconfidence when we allow our judgement to overrule our real ability and experience.

When we, as instructors, certify and turn a new pilot loose on the world, it is our judgement and our hope that he or she has acquired an adequate base level of knowledge, skill, and understanding to safely operate an aircraft as Pilot-In-Command. As we keep saying, the licence in an entry point. It is a "licence to learn".

All of us who fly would like to avoid being part of the sad statistics on aviation accidents. One of the best practices we can develop to help ensure we fly safely is to be very honest with ourselves regarding our abilities: our knowledge, skills, and attitudes.

Yes, do be confident about what you know and can do, but keep in mind as well that confidence must be based on real abilities earned through experience and the development of knowledge and skills. These are won only through time on task, safe attitudes, and an honest appreciation of our own limitations.

NOTES:

Chapter 5.2

Safety Back to the Basics

"Flying is so many parts skill, so many parts planning, so many parts maintenance, and so many parts luck. The trick is to reduce the luck by increasing the others."

-David L. Baker

When we think about aviation safety, we normally consider what we must or can do while flying. Of course, our actions or inactions during flight are very important to flight safety, but they are certainly not the whole story. There are a number of critical steps we might want to consider before we even turn the key or spin the prop to start the aircraft.

Luck may be useful; we certainly don't want to turn it down, but we don't want to rely solely on luck. It's probably a much better plan to take care of what we can as best we can, so we don't have to count on luck to see us through.

If we get right down to the basics, there are three elements involved in flight: the pilot, the machine, and the environment in which the flight will be conducted. All three elements must be taken into consideration prior to commencement of a flight to mitigate the inherent risks.

So what about the pilot? Your life, the lives of your passengers, and the lives of those on the ground beneath you are in your hands. It's important to ensure you are qualified and ready to assume the responsibility of acting as pilot-in-command of a particular aircraft on a particular day.

Based on available accident statistics developed by the Transportation Safety Board in Canada and the National Transportation Safety Board in the United States, pilot error is the cause or a significant, contributing factor in the vast majority of aviation accidents and occurrences.

A safe pilot is the single most important key to safe flight.

Is your licence valid for the intended flight? Is your medical certificate up-to-date? Are you well and healthy and rested? When is the last time you acted as pilot-in-command? Are you current and confident in your own knowledge and skills to operate the particular aircraft you intend to take flying?

If you are not current on the particular aircraft you intend to take to the air, get a checkout with an experienced pilot, someone who has experience with the make and model you intend to fly. Just because a person has 10,000 hours in 757s doesn't mean he or she can slide into the pilot seat of any other aircraft without a proper checkout including a thorough review of the aircraft's POH.

We need to know the machine we will be flying and be familiar with its systems and recommended procedures.

Being correctly licenced, medically validated, and current on the aircraft we intend to fly is still not quite the whole picture. We also need to ensure we are safe to fly TODAY.

The "IMSAFE" list is an excellent item to put on the list of things to check prior to flight. It's a simple checklist of considerations to ensure we are good-to-go.

I: **Illness** - do I have any symptoms?

M: **Medication** - have I been taking any prescription, over-the-counter or any other drugs that might affect my performance?

S: **Stress** - am I under any psychological pressure from my job or home or relationships? Do I have health, family, or money problems that might affect my performance as a pilot?

A: **Alcohol** - have I had anything to drink in the last 24 hours? Do I have a hangover or other post-drinking symptoms that might affect my piloting abilities? Amazingly, NTSB accident reports record that 10% of aviation accidents involve alcohol use as a contributing factor. Which part of, "Don't drink if you are going to fly," is unclear?

F: **Fatigue** - how much time has passed since my last flight? Did I sleep well last night and am I adequately rested and feeling fresh and clear?

E: **Eating** - have I eaten enough of the proper foods to keep me adequately nourished during the entire flight?

Before taking on the responsibility of flight, it is very important to ensure you are happy and healthy, your eyesight is either excellent or corrected to excellent, and you are feeling well, rested, and focused on the particular day you intend to take to the air. Holding a valid medical certificate doesn't ensure we are fit to fly on a given day.

Now that we know whether or not we have a pilot ready for flight, let's consider the aeroplane. For a flight to be conducted safely, the machine we will trust to take us into the air must be properly certified, maintained, inspected, fuelled, and loaded prior to flight.

I've become a bit spoiled in the area of maintenance since most of my flying is in commercially maintained and operated aircraft. I don't want to suggest private aircraft are not often maintained to a very high standard. Most are. Some, however, while meeting the minimum requirements, may not be maintained to the same standard as commercially operated machines.

Typically, privately owned light aircraft fly significantly fewer hours per year than their commercially operated brothers and sisters. A private pilot may fly his or her machine 30 to 50 hours a year on average, and many private aircraft never see anything even close to that amount of flying time from one year to the next. I've seen aircraft come into the shop we use for maintenance for their annual inspection having flown less than 3 hours in the previous year.

While you might suppose that less flying means less wear and tear on an aircraft—and there is some truth to that—sitting for long periods of time can be disastrous to many of an aircraft's components. Avionics, seals, hinges, exhaust systems, cylinders, pistons, electrical systems, and brake systems all suffer considerably if left to sit idle for long periods of time. Sitting idle during the cold and damp winter months is particularly hard on machinery.

If you are flying a commercially maintained rental aircraft, it's not a bad plan to have a chat with the organization's Person Responsible for Maintenance. He or she should be able to answer any questions you may have about a particular aircraft and be able to explain the machine's maintenance program and condition.

If you own and operate your own aircraft, it's an excellent plan to have a good discussion with your AME and get the best possible advice available on setting up an appropriate maintenance schedule for your aircraft based on how it is actually used.

Meeting only the minimum legal requirements may save a few dollars in the short run and may keep you from earning violations, but it may not be a wise choice for either safety or the long-term well being of your machine. Don't put things off any longer than absolutely necessary. Small defects start by being an annoyance but can evolve into a serious nightmare, if ignored.

As the little poster seen in many flying schools indicates, saying or thinking "It won't matter" eventually will.

Of course, just because your machine is on an appropriate maintenance schedule and is all up to date and current doesn't mean it is safe to fly TODAY. Before we even think of starting her up, we want to perform a through pre-flight inspection, including confirming the machine is properly fuelled and loaded within the weight and centre of gravity limits. If you're not quite sure what that means, the aircraft's Pilot Operating Handbook will have some excellent guidelines.

A checkout with a pilot experienced on the particular type can also be very helpful. If there are any difficulties with the machine, the very best place to discover them is on the ground, particularly at your home aerodrome where you have your whole support network just at hand.

The environment in which a flight is to take place—weather and other environmental considerations—is a topic we'll leave for another day, but it is certainly one that does assume a significant importance in our checklist for ensuring safe flight. Weather is at least a contributing factor in a significant number of aviation incidents and accidents. Weather itself, of course, does not cause accidents. However, flying into weather that is beyond a pilot's abilities to conduct safe flight can certainly result in unwanted outcomes.

When thinking about flight safety, it is important to start with the foundational matters: the pilot, the aircraft, and the environment. If we are careful and thorough with the foundation, we set ourselves up for a much better likelihood of success as we proceed with a flight.

NOTES:

Chapter 5.3

Mid-Air Collisions

"What we see depends mainly on what we look for."
                        -Sir John Lubbock, Lord Avebury

"See and avoid" is our key concept in avoiding mid-air collision in a visual reference flight environment. We can only avoid what we can see, and we can only see what we know how to look for.

According to data from a study carried out for the Federal Aviation Administration in 1973, researchers determined that a pilot has an 86% chance of identifying an aircraft the size of a DC-3 six miles distant if he or she is fixating on the target.[4] This is not all that encouraging. There is a lot of sky to scan, and we all know how very small an aircraft appears against the background of big sky.

At a distance of six miles, a distance considered close enough to give a pilot a reasonable opportunity to detect another aircraft, a large aircraft subtends a visual angle of approximately 0.015 degrees. If you want to give yourself a reality check—remember that this is referring to a large aircraft—grab a protractor and see what that looks like.

And, of course, aircraft do not remain fixed in the same location in the air.

Just to toss out some numbers to work with, if we look at two slow general aviation aircraft, a couple of C-152s for example, traveling through the sky at a leisurely 90 knots—1 nautical mile each 40 seconds, a mile and a half per minute—we can calculate their rate of convergence quite easily.

From six miles apart, if the two aircraft are converging head on, they are approaching one another at 180 knots, 1 nautical mile each 20 seconds; they will cover six miles in two minutes (120 seconds). If they are six nautical miles apart and are converging at a 90 degree angle, they will occupy the same piece of airspace in 2.83 minutes (169.7 seconds).

Remember those six miles? It was based on the 86% chance of recognizing and identifying an aircraft the size of a DC-3. It's also based on the idea that the pilot is looking in the right place at the right time. A C-152 occupies quite a bit smaller chunk of the sky and is much less likely to be recognized and identified as easily as a larger aircraft.

The aircraft that presents a risk of collision appears stationary in our windscreen. Its relative position remains constant. Remaining stationary in our visual field adds to the difficulty of detection. Our eyes are much more suited to picking out movement than recognizing fixed objects unless we are looking directly at them, and they are not obscured by a complex background.

Studies show that it takes a pilot approximately 10 seconds to recognize, identify, appreciate the risk of collision with another aircraft, and take appropriate action. This takes a chunk out of our available time. If the aircraft we are flying, or the aircraft converging on our position, is faster than a C-152, our time margins are reduced accordingly.

The key to reducing our risks when flying is to know clearly what the risks are and to know clearly what we need to do to reduce those risks.

Recent studies of mid-air collisions conducted by the National Transportation Safety Board (NTSB) determined that:

- Most aircraft involved in mid-air collisions are involved in recreational flying.
- Most mid-air collisions occurred in VFR weather conditions during weekend daylight hours.
- Most mid-air collisions occurred at or near uncontrolled airports at altitudes below 1000'.
- Pilots of all experience levels from first solo to 20,000-hour veterans were involved in mid-air collisions.
- Flight instructors were on board in 37% of mid-air collisions.
- Most collisions occur in daylight with visibility greater than 3 miles.

So, what can we usefully do to reduce the risk of mid-air collision? There are several, very good ideas we can incorporate into our behaviours to minimize the risk factors. Here are nine very good ideas:

1. Be familiar with the layout of your aircraft and its systems. Pilots who are comfortable and familiar with their aircraft know where things are and do not have to use excess time and energy with their eyes in the cockpit looking for things. In a NASA-funded study, researchers Colvin Kurt and his

colleagues found that some experienced pilots tested spent as much as 68% of their time with their eyes inside the cockpit. As workload increased, time spent looking inside also increased. When your eyes are inside the cockpit, your opportunities for recognizing other aircraft in your area are considerably diminished.

2. Plan your flight ahead and be organized with your navigation and informational materials. The less time you spend referring to materials inside the cockpit, the more time you have available to spend with your eyes outside scanning for potential threats.

3. Keep your aircraft's windows clean and unobstructed. This seems fairly obvious, but how many people conscientiously clean their windows before each flight? How many casually lay maps, flight computers, or other objects on the dash? Dead bugs, water stains, or dirt on the windscreen can be significant contributors to the phenomenon known as Empty Field Myopia; your eyes will tend to use the focal points on the windscreen rather than more distant targets.[5] You effectively become myopic or near-sighted, and an aircraft in your area may be overlooked.

4. Wear sunglasses, as required; do not use opaque sun visors. We all know the effect of glare and the limitations it puts on our ability to see. Using opaque visors can cut down a significant portion of the visible sky and result in failure to recognize a potential collision threat.

5. Always look carefully before manoeuvring your aircraft. Remember all the blind spots—high wing/low wing blockage of view, doorposts, above, below? Whether you are about to turn, climb, or descend a good lookout is an excellent plan.

6. Develop an organized and efficient scanning system and make use of it. Know and understand the limitations of your visual abilities and the blind spots of your particular aircraft. You won't normally find collision threats inside the cockpit; plan to keep your eyes outside engaged in scanning at least 3 times as long as your internal scan. Instructing

your passengers in scanning techniques and encouraging them to report sightings can add an extra degree of safety.

7. Monitor the appropriate frequency for your flight area and make certain you understand what other pilots are saying when they report their positions. Report your own position accurately, as necessary. Be very certain you hear and understand communications from ATC; if you don't understand a transmission for your aircraft, don't be afraid to ask ATC to "Say Again".

8. If you are flying VFR, remain VFR. Don't even think about playing about with a little cloud or two. Your visibility and your see-ability will be drastically reduced.

9. Be very alert when in high traffic areas. Approaching or departing an aerodrome, particularly an uncontrolled aerodrome, puts you in a significantly more vulnerable situation in relation to mid-air collisions: more traffic, limited space, convergence on a particular location and altitude.

Mid-air collisions are not healthy. They are not fun. They should be avoided.

As summer shines down on us, and the sky becomes more crowded, our need to be careful, considerate, and vigilant increases. Appreciating the truth of a risk factor and taking the steps available to minimize that risk can only result in a safer and more enjoyable flight experience.

As David St. George, MCFI, said. "Since more than 80 percent of accidents are pilot error, I argue that the most important airspace is between the pilot's ears."

NOTES:

Chapter 5.4

Emergency Procedures

What is the cause of most aviation accidents?

"Usually it is because someone does too much too soon, followed very quickly by too little too late."

-Steve Wilson
NTSB investigator
Oshkosh, WI, August 1996

It's a beautiful day. You are on a flight from Boundary Bay Airport to Penticton by the lake. Above: the clear blue sky. Below: the majestic peaks of the coast range. What's that smell? Is that burning rubber? Oh, oh. There's smoke seeping out from under the dash.

This is not a good moment to be searching through the POH for a solution.

Modern aircraft are very reliable machines. Accidents and incidents caused by aircraft mechanical failure account for less than 15% of the total number. Of that relatively small percentage, many mechanical failures can be minimized by correct pilot action if that action is undertaken in an organized and timely fashion.

As the Flight Training Manual points out, "As emergencies rarely happen in well-maintained aircraft; their occurrence is usually unexpected. A pilot who is not mentally prepared for an unfamiliar situation may take inappropriate actions to deal with the problem."[6] The Manual goes on to explain the importance of being prepared, having a pre-determined plan of action, and reviewing emergency procedures on a regular basis.

Just as we need to fly on a regular basis to remain current and safe, it is also an excellent idea to review and practice at least the standard emergency procedures applicable to the aircraft we are flying on a regular basis.

School children regularly practice fire and earthquake drills, not in the particular expectation that fires or earthquakes will happen on any regular basis. They practice so that should such an emergency occur, everyone will know exactly what to do and how to do it. The concept is to turn what might be a very dangerous situation into a routine and practiced procedure.

What we hope to accomplish by drill is to turn the recognition of an abnormality and its remedy into a procedure. A procedure is something we can learn and practice. This is the key: a procedure is something we can learn and practice.

When something goes wrong, or doesn't remain right, we have an aircraft abnormality. This can be relatively benign, an irregularity: a fluctuation in a fuel flow gauge, for example, or it can be a serious emergency: a fire in the engine compartment.

An emergency requires both immediate and reference action; an irregularity requires timely reference action. Immediate action items are performed from memory. Reference action items are performed using a written checklist.[7]

Now, let's say we've noticed something isn't right. Before we race off in all directions, remember the big three: Aviate-Navigate-Communicate. The first step is always, no matter what, to gain and maintain control of the aircraft. In simple terms: fly the airplane.

With control of the aircraft established, we can turn our attention to assessing, evaluating, and dealing with the abnormality. If we are faced with an emergency: perhaps a fire or an engine failure, we need to act immediately and from memory.

While a fire is burning is not the time to be fumbling for checklists or the POH.

The procedures for dealing with emergencies must be clear, present in our minds, and the required actions must be quickly and easily performed. That happy state is arrived at only if we have continued to practice and work with the procedures on a regular basis.

The place to get all the required practice with emergency procedures is either sitting in the aircraft on the ground or in an appropriate chair in the comfort of our own home. No sense wasting valuable and expensive airtime with something you can more easily, and much more cheaply, practice on the ground.

Sitting in the aircraft on the ground is an excellent way to practice. Pick an emergency. Imagine what you would hear, what you would see, what you would smell. How would you know that the emergency was taking place? Now, deal with it. Better yet, have a friend or fellow pilot sit with you and announce symptoms rather than naming specific emergencies. Abnormalities have a sneaky way of disguising themselves rather than announcing, "We have a fuel leak." Or, "The right engine is losing power."

At first, using a prepared checklist is a very good idea. Practice makes perfect, but only if you practice the correct actions in the correct order. Be procedural with your response: first step, second step, and so on. Smell the smoke? Electrical fire! Master off; electrical switches off; vents closed; fire extinguisher; vent cabin, and so on.

You can go through the procedure 50 or 100 times until the whole drill is completely automatic. Move the drill from the checklist to your brain to your muscles. Then go on to the next emergency scenario.

If you can do these practice sessions on a regular basis so all the procedures remain fresh, current, and automatic you have done yourself and your passengers a wonderful service. Should an abnormality occur, you are ready and prepared to deal with it in an orderly and procedural manner.

Reference actions are those that are best tackled using our checklist or emergency procedures list. It is also very important to regularly review, be familiar with, and understand the various aircraft systems. Work with your aircraft POH to become familiar with the various systems of your aircraft, the potential abnormalities, their symptoms, and the recommended remedies.

The more prepared we are to deal with abnormal but predictable situations, the less dangerous they will be if they actually occur. In an emergency situation, a few seconds can make a significant difference in the eventual outcome.

Being and staying current, trained, and prepared for unusual or abnormal situations may save not only your life but also the lives of the people who trust you to fly them about the skies.

NOTES:

Chapter 5.5

Single-Pilot Resource Management (SRM)

"We are what we repeatedly do. Excellence, then, is not an act but a habit."

-Aristotle

Aviation safety is always a question of risk management. Each flight involves both risk and benefit. Our job as pilots is to maximize the benefit and manage the inherent risk using the best tools at our disposal. The success of how we go about managing risk and the level of risk we are willing to accept can often be traced back to the type and extent of the training we receive or choose to seek out. As Jay Hopkins wrote, "One of the basic attributes of professionals is that they are always seeking to learn more about their profession."[8]

Single-Pilot Resource Management (SRM), first introduced in 2005 by the National Business Aviation Association[9] and now gaining significant ground in the US, is a system designed to help reduce the number of aviation accidents resulting from human error by teaching pilots about their own limitations and providing training guidelines for single pilots operating the new very light jets (VLJ's). While the system was originally developed for training VLJ pilots, it has rapidly been adapted for other technically advance aircraft (TAA), and it is entirely compatible with the needs of all pilots flying single-pilot aircraft, technically advanced or not.

The principles of SRM apply just as well to the single pilot flying at 60 knots as to the single pilot flying at 250 knots.

Accidents statistics for both GA and commercial operations demonstrate clearly: pilot error is the most common cause of aviation accidents. In the United States, between 70 and 90% of all airline and military aviation accidents are traced back to pilot error.[10] In Canada, pilot error was found to be a "broad cause/factor" in 84% of all aviation accidents and 96% of fatal accidents.[11]

As a good friend of mine likes to say, "The biggest threat to aviation safety is the loose link between the yoke and the rudder pedals."

Most pilots are familiar with the concept of Crew Resource Management (CRM), which focuses on the interactions occurring in the two-crew environment. CRM training has been very successful in reducing the number and frequency of aviation accidents resulting from the difficulties encountered in a multi-crew environment. SRM training is designed to provide the assistance needed by pilots operating in a single crew environment and, just for perspective, in the United States GA accounts for 96% of the total number of aircraft, 60% of the total flight hours, and 94% of the fatal aviation accidents.

In North America, a very significant proportion of all aviation activities and a disproportionate percentage of fatal accidents involve single-pilot operations.[12]

The practical application of SRM centers on what are called the "5 Ps". The 5 Ps are based on the idea that five essential variables impact a pilot's environment and can cause him or her to make a single critical decision or several less critical decisions that, when added together, can create a critical outcome.[13]

The 5 P variables are: the Plan, the Plane, the Pilot, the Passengers, and the Programming.

Using the 5 Ps system, the pilot will review the essential variables of the flight, the 5 Ps, at those points during the flight sequence when decisions are typically most likely to be effective: during the pre-flight planning session; prior to takeoff; at mid point during the flight, unless the flight is longer than two hours, in which case an hourly review is suggested; prior to descent for landing; and just prior to the final approach fix or, if on a VFR flight, just prior to entering the traffic pattern as preparations for landing begin.

Using this system helps the pilot remain alert and aware of the variables that directly affect the safety of the flight, gives him or her scheduled and regular opportunities to review and re-evaluate how the flight is progressing, and to assess whether or not a new plan may be required.

Disciplined use of the 5 Ps is, essentially, a "wake up and smell the coffee" prod for the pilot at each of the critical points in the flight sequence.

The "Plan" contains all the basic elements of cross-country planning including weather, routing, fuel requirements, required publications, and other information. The Plan is not completed and fixed for all time prior to the flight; it must be reviewed on a regular basis as a flight progresses.

Things change: takeoff can be delayed; unexpected changes in the weather may occur; NOTAMS due to forest fires or police activity may be issued; the extra cup of coffee you drank before jumping in the machine may not allow you to continue for the initially planned time of the flight.

While the initial plan stage is a perfect time to evaluate whether or not a flight should be carried out, it is also an ongoing critical variable of the flight that must be reviewed as the flight progresses and new information becomes available.

The "Plane" incorporates all the elements of mechanical and functional aspects of the machine itself. Is the plane capable of the planned flight? Is all maintenance up to date? Do we have sufficient fuel, equipment, avionics, survival supplies, charts, and clothing? In TAA aircraft a review of the Plane expands to include items like database currency, automation status, and emergency backup systems that were not at all common only a few years ago.

Pilot proficiency and currency may also be included when inventorying and reviewing the "Plane" or may be included in the following P, the "Pilot."

The "Pilot" is a critical variable in all flights. Traditionally, most of us have been taught the IMSAFE acronym; it is a good place to start.

Once again, however, a one-time assessment of the pilot, the person on whom all others in the aircraft and all those poor, non-aviating souls walking about below are dependent, is really not sufficient. Just as the weather and the condition of the aircraft change through the duration of the flight, so too does the condition of the pilot. Fatigue, stress, the effects of low altitude hypoxia, and the cumulative effects of noise and vibration all reduce the effectiveness of the person driving the aircraft.

There are reasons why 61% of all aviation accidents occur on landing. At the end of a flight pilot performance is at its lowest point. According to a study carried out by the Bureau of Air Safety Investigation, Department of Transport and Regional Development, the most commonly assigned factor in fatal aviation accidents was poor judgement; judgement is a human capability very susceptible to fatigue.[14]

A review of the condition of the pilot at regular planned intervals during any flight is one excellent way to increase air safety.

The "Passengers" on a flight can also be a critical variable in safety. Particularly for GA and business aviation, passengers can have significant influence over what a pilot does or does not do, and their influence on the pilot can significantly affect how a flight is carried out. The worst-case scenario, perhaps, is when one or more passengers are pilots. There is an old saying: if you ask four rabbis the same question you will get at least 5 answers. The same, no doubt, is true of pilots.

When interacting with non-pilots, the pilot-in-command of the flight must remember passengers do not always understand or appreciate the risks involved in a particular flight. We've all heard some variation on the story of the hunters who wanted to get just one more case of beer or one more trophy deer on the aircraft.

Setting and maintaining a positive and clearly defined relationship between the pilot and passengers is a critical factor in flight safety.

The "Programming", most applicable to TAA aircraft, also has importance for less well-equipped machines. While pilots of TAA aircraft enjoy many benefits from the new technology, that very technology itself can become a challenge. For VFR flight, particularly, pilots may become so engrossed in their screens and devices they become distracted and forget to look outside and maintain positive situational awareness.

Pilots flying TAA aircraft must be very familiar and comfortable with their various devices prior to flight. A good time to learn use of an unfamiliar piece of equipment is on the ground, not during a difficult flight segment.

For all flights, organizing the navigational equipment and instrumentation you will use to assist your efforts to achieve safe flight must be evaluated and re-evaluated at appropriate intervals during the flight, whether that is modern electronic wizardry or maps, watches, and pencils.

In his book, Target Risk 2: A New Psychology of Safety and Health, Gerald J S Wilde, a professor emeritus of psychology at Queen's University in Kingston, Ontario, proposes what he refers to as the Risk Homeostasis theory.[15] The theory of Risk Homeostasis, in short, states that people become accustomed to and comfortable with a particular level of risk. If that level of risk is reduced by some change in the environment, the addition of anti-lock braking systems in cars for example, people tend to respond by driving faster and reducing the distance behind the next vehicle in order to maintain the level of risk with which they are comfortable: people adapt their behaviour to changes in environmental conditions. Few of us willingly embrace change regardless of its form or stated purpose.

As Wilde says, "...safety and lifestyle dependent health is unlikely to improve unless the amount of risk people are willing to take is reduced."[16]

Systematically implementing SRM into a pilot's personal procedures is one way to guide and assist him or her toward becoming more safety conscious and toward consciously reducing the level of risk he or she is willing to accept as normal.

NOTES:

Chapter 5.6

Standard Operating Procedures

"Well-written standard operating procedures (SOPs) provide direction, improve communication, reduce training time, and improve work consistency."

-Richard Stup
Senior Extension Associate
Penn State Dairy Alliance

According to the most recent Transportation Safety Board's summary report of aviation accidents in Canada (2009), general aviation flying continues to show the highest rate of accidents and fatalities for any category of flight activity. Private pilots, over the last ten years, recorded a rate of 20.3 accidents/100,000 hours flown compared with the airlines which recorded an accident rate of only 0.1/100,000 hours flown. [17]

South of the border, General Aviation accident rates are one of the specific items identified in the FAA's top 10 safety concerns.

Transport Canada identifies pilot error as a "broad cause/factor" in 84% of all accidents and 96% of fatal accidents. Modern aircraft maintained to modern standards are quite reliable. As a colleague of mine likes to say, "The major threat to aviation safety is the loose link between the yoke and the rudder pedals." Much of this problem can be traced back to initial and ongoing training practices.

While the accident rates for commercial, airline, and military flight operations have been steadily dropping, the accident rate for General Aviation has remained unacceptably high.

According to the NTSB, "The United States has not had a fatal large commercial aviation accident since February 2009[18], but the story is very different in the world of general aviation (GA). Each year, hundreds of people—450 in 2010—are killed in GA accidents, and thousands more are injured. GA continues to have the highest aviation accident rates within civil aviation: about 6 times higher than small commuter and air taxi operations and over 40 times higher than larger transport category operations. Perhaps what is most distressing is that the causes of GA accidents are almost always a repeat of the circumstances of previous accidents."[19]

Apparently, in GA we are slow to learn our lessons.

One of the key elements in helping reduce and maintain a low accident rate in commercial, airline, and military flying has been the introduction of Crew Resource Management training (CRM) and the use of Standard Operating Procedures (SOPs).

CRM training traces its implementation to a NASA workshop in 1979 that confirmed the primary cause of most aviation accidents is human error. Over the years since, CRM has been integrated in to a wide variety of industries and organizations including aviation; fire service operations; the marine industry, where CRM is referred to as BRM, Bridge Resource Management; hospitals; police operations; and the dairy industry.[20]

In the words of the FAA, "Reducing GA fatality rates require improvements to the aircraft, flying environment, and pilot performance."[21] For those of us involved in the flight training industry, pilot performance stands out as the key element on which to focus our efforts.

Under our current flight training structure, the majority of GA pilot candidates are taught by low time inexperienced instructors in the process of building flight time and experience for themselves on their way to a career in professional aviation. Few of these young men and women, through no fault of their own, have brought to their task of teaching piloting skills the experience of operating in a structured SOP environment, unless their training has been completed at one of the aviation colleges or university programs where that specific training is provided and promoted.

Very few flight-training units outside of the college and university environment, in my observation, include a focus on CRM and the use of SOPs as part of their training programs.

According to the FAA, "Standard operating procedures (SOPs) are universally recognized as basic to safe aviation operations. Effective crew coordination and crew performance, two central concepts of crew resource management (CRM), depend upon the crew's having a shared mental model of each task. That mental model, in turn, is founded on SOPs."[22]

People first entering the world of aviation and seeking training toward private or recreational pilot certificates, young and older, normally walk into that world with little knowledge or ability to evaluate the quality or type of training they will be accepting and paying for. In my own case, I walked into the first flight school I found at a nearby airport and signed up. It was a classic case of, "You pay your nickel and you take your chance."

As Richard Stup so clearly states, "Well-written standard operating procedures (SOPs) provide direction, improve communication, reduce training time, and improve work consistency." When investigating flight training options, an excellent conversation to initiate would be one about training structure and whether or not the school focuses on training for and use of Standard Operating Procedures.

To emphasize the importance of integrating use of SOPs into training programs and operations, I came across one unfortunate example after a very brief search:

On September 16, 2007, at approximately 14:30 hours, a Boeing MD-82 departed Don Mueang International Airport to Phuket International Airport on a domestic flight with 130 crew and passengers on board.

Eighty-seven of those on board were fatally injured in the crash. There were 43 survivors.

After thorough investigation it was determined the probable causes of accident are as follows:

- The flight crew did not follow the Standard Operating Procedure (SOP)...

The team analyzing and reporting on this particular accident identified and highlighted the flight crew's failure to follow SOPs by listing it as the first probable cause of the accident and subsequent loss of life.

When we involved in the flight training industry certify and turn a new pilot loose on the world, it is our judgement and our hope that he or she has acquired an adequate base level of knowledge, skill, and understanding to safely operate an aircraft as Pilot-In-Command.

As we keep saying, the private pilot licence or recreational pilot permit is an entry point. It is a "licence to learn." If that initial training has included a focus on CRM and SOPs, we have laid down a solid foundation for flight safety and a basis for ongoing growth toward expanding competency.

Good habits learned early and well form a solid basis for later learning, safety, and success.

All of us who fly would like to avoid being part of the sad statistics on aviation accidents. One of the best practices we can develop to help ensure we fly safely is to be well trained and consistent in our flight duty performance. This requires solid, initial training in procedural flying, SOPs, and a continuing effort to improve our skills, judgment, and understanding. An ingrained practice of employing SOPs as part of our piloting skills is an important corner stone in building a successful and safe piloting career.

Yes, be confident about what you know and can do, but keep in mind that confidence must be based on real ability earned through experience and the development of knowledge and skills. These are won only through time on task, safe attitudes, and an honest appreciation of our own limitations and a solid initial foundation of training.

First the socks; then the shoes. Each time; every time.

Enjoy.

NOTES:

Chapter 6.1

ABOUT THE AUTHOR

    Alex Burton holds an Airline Transport Licence endorsed for both land and sea, a Class 1 Flight Instructor Rating, and Transport Canada authority as a Pilot Examiner. He has been involved in teaching, managing, and designing educational programs for more than 35 years and has served as Chief Flight Instructor for three Flight Training Units and Chief Pilot for two air charter operations in Canada. He is currently serving as Base Manager for the Selair Pilots Association's satellite training base, in cooperation with the Selkirk College Aviation program, located at the Abbotsford International Airport (CYXX), in Abbotsford, British Columbia. He has been a regular contributor of articles on various aviation topics to national aviation publications both in Canada and in the United States.

Part 7

End Notes

1 Transport Canada, Human Factors for Aviation, Basic Handbook, Transport Canada, pg. 3

2 Transport Canada, Human Factors for Aviation, Basic Handbook, Transport Canada, pg. 5

3 Transport Canada, Human Factors for Aviation, Basic Handbook, Transport Canada, pg. 5

4 Harris, J.L. (1973). Visual aspects of air collision. Visual Search, National Academy of Sciences, Washington, D.C.

5 For a more detailed description of Empty Field Myopia see TP 12863E, Human Factors for Aviation Basic Handbook, pp. 70-71

6 Minister of Public Works and Government Services, Flight Training Manual, 4th Edition Revised, Gage Educational Publishing Company, 1999, p 202.

7 Butcher, Ralph, Haste Makes Waste, AOPA Flight Training Magazine, Aircraft Owners and Pilots Association, December 2003, p 70.

8 Hopkins, Jay. "The Professional Pilot", Flying, Jan 10, 2010.

9 "NBAA Training Guidelines for Single Pilot Operations of Very Light jets and Technically Advanced Aircraft". National Business Aviation Association. 2005, http//www.nbaa.org/ops/safety/vlj/.

10 Wiegmann, D. A., S.A. Shappell (2001), "Human Error Analysis of commercial Aviation Accidents Using the Human Factors analysis and Classification System (HFACS)" (pdf) Federal Aviation Administration.

11 Human Factors for Aviation, Basic Handbook, Transport Canada, pg 3.

12 Kane, Robert (2002), Air Transportation (14th ed.), Kendall/Hunt publishing Company, pp 751, ISBN 0787288810

13 "Managing Risk through Scenario Based Training, Single Pilot Resource Management, and learner Centered Grading," summers, Michele M, Ayers, Frank, Connolly, Thomas; Robertson, Charles,

14 http:/www.narcap.org/articles/ HumanFactorsinFatalAircraftaccidents.pdf

15 Wilde, Gerald J.S. (20001). Target Risk 2: A New Psychology of Safety and Health.

16 Wilde, Gerald J.S. "Risk homeostasis theory: an overview" Injury Prevention 1998; 4:89-91

17 Transportation Safety Board of Canada, Statistical Summary Aviation Occurrences 2009

18 This statistic changed when Asiana Airlines Flight 214 crashed at the San Francisco International Airport in 2013, resulting in the deaths of three passengers.

19 http://www.ntsb.gov/safety/mwl-2.html2

20 Gawande, Atul, The Checklist Manifesto, Metropolitan Books, 2009.

21 http://www.ntsb.gov/safety/mwl-2.html2

22 http://legacy.icao.int/fsix/_Library/AC%20120%2071.pdf

CPSIA information can be obtained at www.ICGtesting.com
Printed in the USA
LVOW08s1539121014

408412LV00003B/389/P